THE WAY
PEOPLE
LIVE

Life in the Negro Baseball Leagues

THE WAY
PEOPLE
LIVE

Life in the Negro Baseball Leagues

Titles in The Way People Live series include:

Cowboys in the Old West
Games of Ancient Rome
Life Aboard a Space Station
Life Aboard the Space Shuttle
Life Among the Aztec
Life Among the Great Plains Indians
Life Among the Ibo Women of Nigeria
Life Among the Inca
Life Among the Indian Fighters
Life Among the Pirates
Life Among the Puritans
Life Among the Samurai
Life Among the Vikings
Life During the American Revolution
Life During the Black Death
Life During the Crusades
Life During the Dust Bowl
Life During the French Revolution
Life During the Gold Rush
Life During the Great Depression
Life During the Middle Ages
Life During the Renaissance
Life During the Roaring Twenties
Life During the Russian Revolution
Life During the Spanish Inquisition
Life in a California Mission
Life in a Japanese American Internment
   Camp
Life in a Medieval Castle
Life in a Medieval Monastery
Life in a Medieval Village
Life in America During the 1960s
Life in an Amish Community
Life in a Nazi Concentration Camp
Life in Ancient Athens
Life in Ancient China
Life in Ancient Egypt
Life in Ancient Greece
Life in Ancient Rome

Life in a Wild West Show
Life in Berlin
Life in Castro's Cuba
Life in Charles Dickens's England
Life in Communist Russia
Life in Genghis Khan's Mongolia
Life in Hong Kong
Life in Moscow
Life in the Amazon Rain Forest
Life in the American Colonies
Life in the Australian Outback
Life in the Elizabethan Theater
Life in the Hitler Youth
Life in the Negro Baseball Leagues
Life in the North During the Civil War
Life in the South During the Civil War
Life in the Warsaw Ghetto
Life in Tokyo
Life in War-Torn Bosnia
Life of a Medieval Knight
Life of a Nazi Soldier
Life of a Roman Gladiator
Life of a Roman Slave
Life of a Roman Soldier
Life of a Slave on a Southern
   Plantation
Life on Alcatraz
Life on a Medieval Pilgrimage
Life on an African Slave Ship
Life on an Everest Expedition
Life on a New World Voyage
Life on an Indian Reservation
Life on Ellis Island
Life on the American Frontier
Life on the Oregon Trail
Life on the Pony Express
Life on the Underground Railroad
Life Under the Jim Crow Laws
Life Under the Taliban

THE WAY
PEOPLE
LIVE

Life
in the Negro
Baseball
Leagues

by John F. Wukovits

LUCENT BOOKS

An imprint of Thomson Gale, a part of The Thomson Corporation

THOMSON
—————— ™
GALE

Detroit • New York • San Francisco • San Diego • New Haven, Conn. • Waterville, Maine • London • Munich

LIBRARY OF CONGRESS CATALOGING-IN-PUBLICATION DATA

Wukovits, John F., 1944–
  Life in the Negro Baseball Leagues / by John F. Wokovits.
    p. cm. — (The way people live)
  Includes bibliographical references and index.
  ISBN 1-59018-273-1 (hard cover : alk. paper)
Summary: Discusses aspects of the life in the Negro baseball leagues, including recruitment, training, obstacles, opportunities, as well as the values of their day.
  1. Baseball—Juvenile literature. 2. African Americans—Juvenile literature. I. Title.
II. Series.

Printed in the United States of America

Contents

Discovering the Humanity in Us All

Books in The Way People Live series focus on groups of people in a wide variety of circumstances, settings, and time periods. Some books focus on different cultural groups, others on people in a particular historical time period, while others cover people involved in a specific event. Each book emphasizes the daily routines, personal and historical struggles, and achievements of people from all walks of life.

To really understand any culture, it is necessary to strip the mind of the common notions we hold about groups of people. These stereotypes are the archenemies of learning. It does not even matter whether the stereotypes are positive or negative; they are confining and tight. Removing them is a challenge that is not easily met, as anyone who has ever tried it will admit. Ideas that do not fit into the templates we create are unwelcome visitors—ones we would prefer remain quietly in a corner or forgotten room.

The cowboy of the Old West is a good example of such confining roles. The cowboy was courageous, yet soft-spoken. His time (it is always a he, in our template) was spent alternatively saving a rancher's daughter from certain death on a runaway stagecoach, or shooting it out with rustlers. At times, of course, he was likely to get a little crazy in town after a trail drive, but for the most part, he was the epitome of inner strength. It is disconcerting to find out that the cowboy is human, even a bit childish. Can it really be true that cowboys would line up to help the cook on the trail drive grind coffee, just hoping he would give them a little stick of peppermint candy that came with the coffee shipment? The idea of tough cowboys vying with one another to help "Coosie" (as they called their cooks) for a bit of candy seems silly and out of place.

So is the vision of Eskimos playing video games and watching MTV, living in prefab housing in the Arctic. It just does not fit with what "Eskimo" means. We are far more comfortable with snow igloos and whale blubber, harpoons and kayaks.

Although the cultures dealt with in Lucent's The Way People Live series are often historically and socially well known, the emphasis is on the personal aspects of life. Groups of people, while unquestionably affected by their politics and their governmental structures, are more than those institutions. How do people in a particular time and place educate their children? What do they eat? And how do they build their houses? What kinds of work do they do? What kinds of games do they enjoy? The answers to these questions bring these cultures to life. People's lives are revealed in the particulars and only by knowing the particulars can we understand these cultures' will to survive and their moments of weakness and greatness.

This is not to say that understanding politics does not help to understand a culture. There is no question that the Warsaw ghetto, for example, was a culture that was brought about by the politics and social ideas of Adolf

Hitler and the Third Reich. But the Jews who were crowded together in the ghetto cannot be understood by the Reich's politics. Their life was a day-to-day battle for existence, and the creativity and methods they used to prolong their lives is a vital story of human perseverance that would be denied by focusing only on the institutions of Hitler's Germany. Knowing that children as young as five or six outwitted Nazi guards on a daily basis, that Jewish policemen helped the Germans control the ghetto, that children attended secret schools in the ghetto and even earned diplomas—these are the things that reveal the fabric of life, that can inspire, intrigue, and amaze.

Books in The Way People Live series allow both the casual reader and the student to see humans as victims, heroes, and onlookers. And although humans act in ways that can fill us with feelings of sorrow and revulsion, it is important to remember that "hero," "predator," and "victim" are dangerous terms. Heaping undue pity or praise on people reduces them to objects, and strips them of their humanity.

Seeing the Jews of Warsaw only as victims is to deny their humanity. Seeing them only as they appear in surviving photos, staring at the camera with infinite sadness, is limiting, both to them and to those who want to understand them. To an object of pity, the only appropriate response becomes "Those poor creatures!" and that reduces both the quality of their struggle and the depth of their despair. No one is served by such two-dimensional views of people and their cultures.

With this in mind, The Way People Live series strives to flesh out the traditional, two-dimensional views of people in various cultures and historical circumstances. Using a wide variety of primary quotations—the words not only of the politicians and government leaders, but of the real people whose lives are being examined—each book in the series attempts to show an honest and complete picture of a culture removed from our own by time or space.

By examining cultures in this way, the reader will notice not only the glaring differences from his or her own culture, but also will be struck by the similarities. For indeed, people share common needs—warmth, good company, stability, and affirmation from others. Ultimately, seeing how people really live, or have lived, can only enrich our understanding of ourselves.

Two Realms

One look at a current major league baseball roster reveals players of all races and colors, creeds and backgrounds. This has been true for so long that many people find it hard to believe that, at one not-so-distant time, unwritten rules and codes of behavior excluded a large segment of society from America's pastime. African Americans, who have contributed amazing exploits and established remarkable records, watched from the outside from 1887 until 1947, when Jackie Robinson finally broke the barrier separating white from black baseball.

Adding insult to injury is the fact that while African Americans had to stage their contests in the shadow of the white major leagues, most of their feats have gone unnoticed by many. Hitters with the prowess to match Babe Ruth and pitchers whose blazing fastballs equaled the top flamethrowers in the major leagues worked in relative anonymity, recognized only by their black baseball brethren, African American fans, and a handful of white admirers.

The Origins of Blackball

According to tradition, Gen. Abner Doubleday started baseball in 1839 in Cooperstown, New York. In baseball's early years, free black athletes joined white players on integrated teams in the East and Midwest. Blackball, the term commonly applied to contests between two black teams, started on September 28, 1860, when the Weeksville squad from New York defeated the Colored Union Club of New York 11–0. Seven years later the first champi-onship game pitted the Brooklyn Uniques against the Philadelphia Excelsiors.

In 1884 Moses Fleetwood Walker became the first African American to play major league baseball when his Toledo minor league squad joined the American Association, then a major league. His presence sparked immediate protest from white players and set a bitter tone that would dominate baseball well into the next century.

"The Equal to Any White Players"

Frank Thompson organized the first renowned black professional baseball squad, the Babylon Athletics, in 1885. A headwaiter at the Argyle Hotel, a luxurious Long Island resort that catered to wealthy whites who fled New York City's sweltering summer heat, Thompson collected a group of black employees and staged baseball contests against local clubs to entertain white guests. When the resort closed for the winter, Thompson took his club to warmer climes and barnstormed—played games against any opposition he could find, major or minor league teams, college squads from Princeton and Yale, or local clubs assembled by small towns—through the South and West.

To arrange additional games against white major league talent, Thompson changed the team name to the Cuban Giants. While some white players objected to stepping onto the same field with blacks, for some reason they had few qualms if they thought their opponents came from Cuba.

Thompson's band quickly developed a reputation as the most talented black team in the country. In 1887 they had the World Series champion Detroit Tigers on the ropes, leading 4–2 in the eighth inning, when four errors allowed the Tigers to win. So many offers flooded in from other teams hoping to pit their best nine against the Giants that the club could select its opposition. Thompson placed ads stating, "The Cuban Giants are now desirous of hearing from all the leading clubs in the country traveling this way, as we can pay good guarantees to first-class clubs."[1]

A military officer during the Mexican War and the Civil War, Abner Doubleday (pictured in 1865 with his wife) is traditionally credited with inventing the game of baseball.

He also paid his own players well, handing out paychecks for as much as eighteen dollars per week at a time when the cost of attending a picture show was less than ten cents and one could buy a roast beef and mashed potato meal, complete with coffee and pie, at a four-star restaurant for eighty-five cents.

Hoping to imitate their success, other black squads started to barnstorm, but before the turn of the century none matched the reputation of the Cuban Giants for professionalism. Many white teams declined invitations to challenge the Cuban Giants out of fear of being humiliated, and other black teams included the word "Giant" in their names to take advantage of the team's popularity. "There are players among these colored men that are the equal to any white players on the ballfield," proclaimed the *Sporting News* in 1888. "If you don't think so, go and see the Cuban Giants play. This club, with its strongest players on the field, would play a favorable game against such clubs as the New Yorks or Chicagos."[2]

By the late 1880s, black squads had been formed in many large cities east of the Mississippi River. While most played a straightforward game, without other attractions to draw out fans, in 1895 the Page Fence Giants of Adrian, Michigan, added a new wrinkle by parading on bicycles through town to advertise that afternoon's game. Future teams would take that tendency to new heights in the next century.

In 1884 Moses Fleetwood Walker became the first African American to play major league baseball.

"How Far Will This Mania Go?"

For the black ballplayer, however, hand in hand with first-rate baseball came second-rate treatment. People in the late 1800s recalled the bitterness engendered by slavery and the resulting Civil War—many themselves had, in fact, toiled under the hot sun and stinging whip as a slave or grappled hand-to-hand in mortal combat as a soldier. Unchecked bigotry pervaded much of the land, and one world it affected was that of major league baseball.

In December 1867, only two years after the Civil War, the National Association of Base Ball Players voted to exclude any team that employed black athletes. Although blacks played in other leagues, including the majors, before 1900, the trend quickly veered toward exclusion.

Some accounts state that by the mid-1880s, as many as sixty blacks played on mixed squads. Due to inadequate record keeping, only eight can be verified, including the now-legendary George Stovey and Moses Fleetwood Walker, but the higher number is likely more accurate. Like the men who would follow, these pioneers faced obstacles above and beyond those normally presented by baseball at the top levels.

Page Fence Giants

The Page Fence Giants, one of the earliest professional black baseball teams, influenced their sport from the time of their origin in Adrian, Michigan, in 1895. Sponsored by the white owners of the Page Woven Wire Fence Company, a business that produced new fencing used to confine livestock, the Page Fence Giants played their games on the road, since they lacked a home field. The traveling did not seem to bother them, as they compiled an envious record. In 1895, they won 118 games and lost only 36 against teams ranging from local talent to major league opposition. They played two games against an all-star squad formed from the majors, and defeated them both times, 18–3 and 15–0, leading one newspaper to label the Page Fence Giants the best team in Michigan.

Thanks to their success and the profits of their owner, the players rode in a custom-built sixty-foot-long Pullman railroad car, complete with cooks and porters, instead of riding in antiquated buses. When they arrived in a town, the team frequently organized a parade and gaily marched to the field, where they usually proceeded to dismantle the competing nine.

The Page Fence Giants pose with rolls of Page Woven Wire fences for a publicity photo in the late 1890s.

Moses Fleetwood Walker faced heckling and threatening letters whenever his Toledo team played in the South. White pitchers purposely threw at his head more frequently than they did to white batters, and some teammates refused to sit for team pictures with their black cohorts.

Black pitcher Joe Simmons faced a perplexing quandary in an 1887 game when his white fielders committed obvious errors in an effort to undermine him. They acted so outrageously that the *Toronto World* condemned their disgusting performance and praised Simmons for reacting in a calm manner.

Second baseman Bud Fowler strapped wood splints over his shins because so many whites tried to spike him when they slid in to the base. One white player commiserated on Fowler's predicament and told *Sporting Life* in 1889,

While I myself am prejudiced against playing on a team with a colored player, still I could not help pitying some of the poor black fellows. . . . I have seen [Bud Fowler] muff balls intentionally, so that he would not have to try to touch runners, fearing they might injure him. [Frank] Grant was

Pictured in 1885 with the Keokuk Kernels of Iowa, Bud Fowler (back row, center) was one of the first black athletes to play organized baseball.

Early in the history of black baseball, a few white owners unsuccessfully tried to circumvent the color barrier. In 1901 the two main major leagues, the American League and the National League, started an all-out bidding war for the services of talented whites. Clubs scrambled for players, hoping to land the top batters and pitchers before their opposition.

John J. McGraw, manager of the Baltimore Orioles, thought he saw a way to include one of the best black athletes of his day, the light-skinned Charlie Grant. McGraw hoped that he could pass Grant as a Cherokee warrior. According to the story, McGraw studied a map, saw a creek named Tokohama, and told Grant that he was now Chief Tokohama.

His ruse failed to fool anyone, however. Charles Comiskey, owner of the Chicago White Sox, led the charge to ban Grant. As Robert W. Peterson relates in his 1970 book, *Only the Ball Was White*, Comiskey warned, "I'm not going to stand for McGraw ringing in an Indian on the Baltimore team. If Muggsy really keeps this Indian, I will get a Chinaman of my acquaintance and put him on third. Somebody told me that the Cherokee of McGraw's is really Grant, the crack Negro second baseman from Cincin-

Charlie Grant, a light-skinned African American, posed as a Cherokee warrior in order to play with the Baltimore Orioles.

nati, fixed up with war paint and a bunch of feathers."

This and other objections forced McGraw to pull Grant from his team before Baltimore opened season play.

the same way. Why, the runners chased him off second base. [3]

However, most sentiments in the magazine shared the feeling expressed by an 1887 article in *Sporting Life* that asked, "How far will this mania for engaging colored players go? At the present rate of progress the Inter-national League ere many months may change its title to 'Colored League.'" [4]

The Color Line Is Drawn

The magazine's lament received a quick response. On July 14 of the same year, one of baseball's white legends, player-manager Cap Anson, refused to field his Chicago White Stockings against the Newark Little Giants unless Newark benched its two stars, black players George Stovey and Moses Fleetwood Walker. Newark caved in to Anson.

That same day, the ten teams comprising the International League met in Buffalo to discuss the issue of black athletes in the league. Worried that they would lose some of their top white talent because of animosity toward blacks, the teams voted to exclude blacks from future play. With that decision, an unofficial color line was drawn that spread to other leagues. Team owners operated under an unwritten, but clearly understood, rule to assemble white-only squads. By 1900, blacks had been banned from major and minor league baseball.

Out of necessity, black athletes turned to other arenas of competition. With the majors and minors now forbidden territory, blacks formed their own teams and leagues.

Until Jackie Robinson smashed the color barrier in 1947, baseball at the highest level thus operated in two realms, white and black. African Americans developed a lively, fertile realm of their own that offered drama, excitement, and stellar performances.

"I Learned Baseball the Hard Way"

Black baseball offered two venues in which players showcased their talents. Barnstorming tours, which provided the main source of livelihood, pitted teams of African Americans against the best local talent during tours of the American countryside. The second venue, league play, offered a stability and structure that barnstorming could not yield.

Making It to the Big Leagues

The route to the top teams for a black athlete was much the same as for a white athlete hoping to make it to the majors—someone had to notice his talent and offer him a position. Like their white counterparts, thousands of black youths played baseball whenever they could. Wilmer Fields, a member of the famed Homestead Grays squad in the 1930s, rushed to a nearby vacant lot every day with his friends in Manassas, Virginia, and, using a tennis ball or even a rag ball, staged contests all summer long.

To become professionals, Fields and the countless other hopefuls had to depend on making a quick impression on a visiting black professional team, since black leagues could not afford a network of scouts. Either they played well against the professionals when their shot arose, and possibly received an invitation to try out for the organization, or they abandoned hopes of making it. Ray Dandridge impressed the Detroit Stars when they visited his hometown of Portsmouth, Virginia, in 1933 and played a local team of factory workers and dockyard laborers. After Dandridge smashed a home run and showed a deft touch in the field, the Stars' manager convinced Dandridge's parents to allow their nineteen-year-old son to join them for the rest of the season. In 1925 Chet Brewer, a standout high school football and baseball star from Des Moines, Iowa, signed with the Monarchs after a similar favorable showing. Two hours after defeating a top professional team, pitcher Dave Barnhill received two hundred dollars, a train ticket, and a telegram asking him to join them.

Other individuals joined a professional team as a replacement for an injured star or for a pro battling a slump. A select handful first made their mark for renowned black colleges such as Howard, Lincoln, or the Tuskegee Institute; played for exceptional high school squads; or competed in the tough industrial leagues, which scheduled games of workers from factories and mills against each other. Southern sawmills and mines produced particularly talented groups of black baseball players.

Parents often assumed a role in supporting their sons' athletic aspirations. Dave Malarcher, who starred from 1916 to 1935, played baseball for hours as a youth, usually wearing a uniform handmade by his mother. He and other boys from his town competed against teams from neighboring cities, often playing after pulling weeds in rice fields on Saturdays. When a professional team spotted

In 1939 Wilmer Fields was recruited to play for the Washington Homestead Grays at the age of seventeen.

greats, and heralded track star and team owner Jesse Owens visited Connie Johnson's mother in a quest to gain her permission to sign her son. She listened, then made the pair promise they would take care of her son before lending her assent.

Other black youths had to take more drastic action. Jake Stephens's father forbade him to join a professional team, so one night Jake waited until his parents fell asleep, climbed down the back balcony, and scampered into the night to begin his professional career. George Giles simply walked into a hotel where the Kansas City Monarch players were staying and asked them how to become a professional. They told him to join their tryouts the following spring. He did, and made the team.

John "Buck" O'Neil overcame great obstacles to join the professional ranks, since the Sarasota, Florida, area in which he grew up did not even have a high school for blacks. He frequently walked past the white high school, looked at his mother, and said, with considerable understatement, "It's kinda bad I can't go there."[5] Through the intercession of a friend, however, O'Neil moved to Jacksonville, excelled at high school baseball before joining a Methodist college squad, then signed with a professional team.

The route to professional baseball varied with each individual. When they arrived, they found that the sport offered a path to an improved future.

League Play

Once a young ballplayer reached the professional ranks, he participated year-round in two separate arenas. Barnstorming tours occurred throughout much of the year, and from February until September, the more structured Negro baseball leagues provided competition.

him in a 1916 exhibition match, they offered him fifty dollars a month, money Malarcher faithfully sent home to his mother, who had been born a slave. Player-manager Oscar Charleston, one of black baseball's all-time

League play owed its existence to three capable black businessmen. In 1920 Rube Foster, the father of the Negro leagues, formed the first of three confederations that lasted, with brief interruptions during the Depression of the 1930s, until 1960. His Negro National League handed players and fans a regular schedule of games and a stability that barnstorming lacked. Teams such as the Chicago American Giants, Detroit Stars, Hilldale of Philadelphia, and the most renowned of all, the Kansas City Monarchs, embarked on schedules that brought the top black teams to the most populated centers on a regular basis.

Cumberland Willis Posey, a Penn State graduate whose grandfather had been a slave, financed another distinguished collection, the Homestead Grays, while Gus Greenlee, who had started his career in the illegal numbers betting racket, helped the leagues survive the economically troubled 1930s. Greenlee, an astute businessman, also instituted the vehicle that eventually brought the most national exposure to black baseball talent, the annual East-West all-star game.

Negro leagues flourished in northern metropolises such as New York and Chicago, as well as areas containing a large population of African Americans, such as Pittsburgh and Newark, New Jersey. At a time when segregation dramatically limited opportunities for black businessmen, league play also offered one of the few chances for such men to excel, and before long black-owned baseball teams became one of the largest enterprises in the years before segregation ended.

"Every Day We Went Out There to Play"

Like the white major leagues, the Negro leagues started each season with spring training. That was about the only similarity, though. Teams opened spring training in the South, but after only a few days of working out and executing drills, the black ballplayers hit the road on barnstorming tours. Better-funded white teams could allow the players six to eight weeks of training with numerous practice games, but the Negro teams had to arrange income-producing matches in the first week to help pay the bills.

"No sooner did you pull on your uniform than you were in a game, playing before paying customers,"[6] related catcher Roy Campanella.

Working Their Way Up

Unlike the white professional ballplayer, who enjoyed the benefits of a scouting system and organized minor leagues to channel the best players to the majors, black athletes had no convenient ladder to the big leagues. They played hard, then hoped a break would come. In his 1983 book, *Invisible Men: Life in Baseball's Negro Leagues,* Donn Rogosin explained many vehicles that funneled young boys toward the professional ranks:

"There were thus many roads to the Negro leagues; players came from the North and South, cities and farms, sandlots and industrial teams, and from the entire Caribbean basin. In every part of America where blacks lived in any numbers, there were black teams, and everywhere baseball was the number-one sports spectacle. In schools, factories, church leagues, and on the sandlots, baseball was 'it.' Therefore, making it into the Negro leagues was an extraordinary accomplishment. The players who negotiated that journey represented the tip of a black sports pyramid which reached into every black community in the nation."

Of all the great figures to populate black baseball, one of the most influential was Andrew "Rube" Foster. He made marks not only on the playing field, where he pitched with authority, but as a manager, owner, and most importantly, organizer of the Negro leagues.

Born in the farm town of Calvert, Texas, in 1879, Foster was a master at psychology. He was known for smiling at the batter in tough situations, or to purposely take his time on the mound when a hitter appeared anxious to swing at the ball. He claimed that surprise, more than anything, defeated the opposition, so he tried to do what the other team least expected.

Foster also gained distinction with his managerial skills. His teams usually ended with superlative records, topped by his 1910 American Giants, which won 123 of 129 contests. He scorned no trick to attain a victory, even resorting to drenching his infield the night before games so his speedy batters could bunt balls that infielders had trouble reaching.

He also demanded his players follow orders. In *Only the Ball Was White*, Robert W. Peterson relates a story told by Foster's son, Earl:

"One time Jelly Gardner was sent up to bunt and he tripled. He came back and sat down on the bench. The old man [Foster] took that pipe he smoked—he always had it—and he popped him right across the head. And he fined him and told him, 'As long as I'm paying you, you'll do as I tell you to do.'"

Foster's greatest accomplishment, however, came in 1920 when he organized the Negro leagues. This guaranteed a decent wage for the athletes, ended a disastrous string of raids in which rival teams enticed one another's players, and set standards for decent behavior. Foster ensured that black baseball would continue, at least until that distant day when the major leagues accepted black athletes.

After a lengthy illness, including stays in mental institutions, Foster died in December 1930. Called the "Father of Black Baseball," Foster was named to the Hall of Fame in 1981.

Andrew "Rube" Foster, often called the "Father of Black Baseball," organized the Negro National League in 1920.

Fielders and batters played themselves into shape rather than relying on the slower-paced training schedule that existed in the white leagues. Fortunately, since most black athletes played baseball year-round, few had to worry about their physical conditioning.

The Homestead Grays scheduled no more than six days of conditioning before swinging right into their first of many contests over the next two months. They played games throughout the South, often with college nines, and barnstormed their way north as the weather improved. Sometimes, two teams traveled the same migratory route out of the South, sharing expenses along the way.

Since the Negro leagues lacked full-time coaches, again due to insufficient finances, younger players had to learn the game by listening, observing, and imitating. Even the team manager doubled as a player and could spare little time to instruct rookies or other team members. Walter "Buck" Leonard, who played from 1933 to 1950 for many teams, including the Homestead Grays, said,

> We didn't have time to teach to young ballplayers coming up. Every day we went out there to play, and we didn't have coaches. We just had pitchers who pitched the day before to coach at third and first. We didn't have paid coaches and all like that, and the manager was playing in the outfield or some other position. He wasn't sitting on the bench until our later years.[7]

Leonard, a superb fastball hitter who struggled with change-of-pace pitches early in his career, learned how to adjust to the slower pitch through experience. He could not turn to a coach to help him, as a white player in the majors could do.

Spring training ended when teams arrived north in late April or early May for the regular league opener. This first contest packed stadiums and brought out noted black entertainers and politicians. Men and women attended in their finest clothes, parades heralded the game's arrival, and even white politicians appeared, sensing votes in the enormous crowds.

"Oh boy, did they dress," stated Effa Manley, who with her husband owned and operated black teams in the 1930s and 1940s. "People came out who didn't know the ball from the bat. All the girls got new outfits."[8]

One 1937 opening day contest in Chicago featured a parade of five hundred cars, a high school marching squad, two fifty-piece bands, and a contingent from the Veterans of Foreign Wars. Throngs followed the parade's progress through the streets and toward the stadium, where they brought in a fresh season by cheering their home team on.

Iron Men of Baseball

Another difference between the white and black leagues was the size of the teams. Twenty-five athletes played for the New York Yankees, the Detroit Tigers, and other white teams, while, in an effort to reduce costs, most black organizations limited the number to between thirteen and fifteen players. Individuals specialized in playing multiple positions, and pitchers knew that they would frequently work both games of a doubleheader. Usually, the top eight athletes played every day, one of the two or three pitchers headed to the mound, and the other two or three substitutes rode the bench until an injury or deep slump handed them an opportunity to play.

Since they had to pitch so often, pitchers turned to junk balls and illegal pitches faster than in the white major leagues, where hurlers played only once every four games. Batters knew they would face an array of spit balls, which madly

A long line of African American fans waits to enter Engel Stadium in Tennessee to watch a Negro leagues game.

fluctuated in their path to the plate, or balls that the pitcher had surreptitiously cut or scraped on a rough surface, such as a hidden bottle cap, giving him a better grip with which to throw a curveball. "I've had balls come in on the heart of the plate; when I'd swing it would be over my head,"[9] said outfielder Gene Benson.

Black athletes generally claimed that Negro league squads equaled the highest minor league talent in white baseball. They contended that enough superb stars existed in the leagues to form two or three teams that could easily have competed against the New York Yankees or Boston Red Sox, but because of a lack of depth, the Negro leagues as a whole were outmatched. "We didn't have star men at every position," explained Leonard. "We didn't have—as the majors did—two good catchers and six or seven good pitchers and good infielders and outfielders."[10]

Men played hurt more often, remained in games longer, and sometimes saw action in as many as four games a day. White sportswriter Damon Runyon marveled at the resiliency shown by black athletes. In 1932 he watched Ted Radcliffe catch the great Satchel Paige for the Pittsburgh Crawfords in the opening game of a doubleheader. After a brief intermission, Radcliffe then walked to the mound and tossed a nine-inning, 5–0 shutout in the second contest.

"The Negro Leagues Made Me"

Life in the Negro leagues for black athletes often meant erratic scheduling. Forced to rent stadiums, since few teams had the financial backing to construct their own, team owners took whatever days and times were available after white teams had used the field. For a percentage of the gate, such venerable sites as New York's Yankee Stadium and St. Louis's Sportsman's Park opened their doors to black players, who drew crowds in excess of forty thousand for weekend games. As a result, though, few black teams played the same number of games each year in league competition. In 1921, for instance, the American Giants played sixty-two games and won the pennant, while the second-place Kansas City Monarchs suited up for eighty-one contests.

Inevitably, the Negro leagues had trouble placing every team in a ballpark. Some organizations faced the awkward position of playing

Ted "Double Duty" Radcliffe (far left) earned his nickname for his ability to play both as a catcher and as a pitcher.

White spectators watch a Kansas City Monarchs game at Muehleback Stadium. Kansas City was one of the few teams in the Negro leagues to have a home stadium.

an entire season as road teams because they could not find a ballpark available in their home area. The haphazard scheduling also meant that most games occurred either in the later afternoon or early evening, when the white teams had finished. Black athletes thus battled darkness as well as their opponent, at least until lights arrived in the 1930s.

Other hardships plagued black baseball that the white major leagues never worried about. To cut costs, umpires tossed out very few baseballs, even those that were haggard and scraped. Kids chased after home run balls, not so much for a souvenir, but for the free tickets they re-

ceived as enticement for returning the ball. Only the heaviest downpours canceled contests, for a washout resulted in serious financial loss to the teams involved. Home teams, rather than the league, provided umpires, resulting in uneven quality from stop to stop and charges of favoritism for the home squad. Lloyd "Pepper" Bassett, who starred for seven teams from 1934–1950, claimed of the poorly trained officials, "there was no umpiring, only guesses."[11]

The officials may not have measured up, but the players took their contests seriously. Dick Seay, whose career spanned three decades, said about base runners sliding into fielders, "If your mother's playing second base they'd tell ya, run her over."[12]

The same attitude carried to the mound. Should any batter nudge too close to the plate, he likely had to duck on the following pitch. "Out on the mound you were my enemy," said pitcher Connie Johnson. "After the game we go out together, eat together, laugh together, have a good time, but not out on that mound, the smiling's gone."[13]

Judy Johnson, rated by many as the greatest third baseman in Negro league ball, often had his uniform torn by players who slid in with their spikes flashing. A manager admonished first baseman George Giles that he had better have a thick skin: "If you don't have guts, they'll run you home to momma."[14]

All this made life in professional baseball tougher for black players than it was for Babe Ruth, Ted Williams, or other white players. The schedule, added to the constant barnstorming games, lengthy road trips, and substandard living conditions, could be so exhausting that Willie Mays, who started in the Negro leagues before embarking on a Hall of Fame career with the New York/San Francisco Giants, claimed that "the major leagues were easy for me. I learned baseball the hard way; the Negro leagues made me."[15]

Decent Pay

Despite the difficulties, players in the Negro leagues enjoyed something that few black athletes possessed—a stable wage. Players had been guaranteed a salary since the inception of the Negro National League in 1920.

In sound economic times, a wage of $400 per month was not uncommon, and even the lowest-paid players, who received $175 per month, lived better than most black workers in other fields. The pay, along with anything else they could earn barnstorming or playing winter ball, meant that many players in the Negro leagues did not have to work at other jobs to support themselves. Players who could not land a position in winter ball returned to factories or farms to supplement their incomes. Legendary pitcher Satchel Paige was the highest-paid player in the leagues with an annual salary reaching $40,000 in the 1930s. Home run hitter Josh Gibson, called the black Babe Ruth, earned $1,000 a month for the six-month season.

During the Depression of the 1930s, as with many other occupations, payday was often an adventure. Instead of a paycheck, clubs sometimes offered to divide the gate receipts among the players. Even when salaries dropped

The Negro Leagues

To most Americans, accustomed to the long-standing existence of two major leagues, the hectic coming and going of leagues in Negro baseball is surprising. Rube Foster started the first league in 1920 with the Negro National League. Three years later, the Eastern Colored League opened play, but lasted only until 1928. By 1931, with the Depression affecting most enterprises, the Negro National League folded, returning two years later under the guidance of Gus Greenlee. Five years after that, the Negro American League opened, once again giving Negro baseball two solid divisions. This situation lasted until 1948, when the Negro National League disbanded following Jackie Robinson and the breaking of the color barrier. The Negro American League, a mere shadow of its former self, hung on until 1960, when it, too, disappeared into history.

during the Depression, players could hardly complain, since many of their countrymen were out of work.

"One of His Musts"

Like the white players, black baseball stars served as role models to thousands of youths around the country. Chet Brewer, who later played for the Kansas City Monarchs, watched every team that traveled to his hometown of Des Moines, Iowa. He and his buddies climbed a tree behind the left field fence to watch his idol, Bullet Joe Rogan, blaze fastballs by hitters. Brewer realized his dream when he joined the Negro leagues in 1925.

James "Cool Papa" Bell not only accumulated Hall of Fame numbers, but so influenced a young Roy Campanella that he, too, played his way into baseball's Hall of Fame. Bell recalled of the youngster who later gained fame as an all-star catcher for the Brooklyn Dodgers,

I used to let Roy Campanella and his team in the ball park when he was a little kid in

Josh Gibson slides across home plate during a 1944 game. Gibson was one of the highest paid players in the Negro leagues.

Philadelphia around 1933. Campanella played on a team called the Metros, and I took them to the ball park. Not the whole team; about four or five little boys. I told the man, "These are ballplayers, let 'em in." I said, "They haven't got any money, but they'll grow up to be men and they'll be baseball fans.[16]

Team owners knew how influential their players could be on the younger generation, so they demanded courteous behavior and proper dress off the field. When Paul Stevens tried out for the Hilldale club, he realized he had made the team when the owner accompanied him to a local clothing store and purchased two suits and two hats for him.

Monarchs owner J.L. Wilkinson set rigid standards for his players. Othello Renfroe recalled,

They could tell some tall tales about ball players they picked up in these little country towns who would come out and pitch with football shoes on or tennis shoes, and they could throw a ball so hard. The Kansas City Monarchs were very good at that, picking up guys in little small towns in Texas and Arkansas and taking them to town and buying them clothes, you know, guys who didn't even know what a suit of clothes was. But Mr. Wilkinson made sure that you dressed well. That was one of his musts.[17]

In the 1920s some parents still objected to their boys playing professional baseball because they believed that only people of low reputation engaged in the sport on a full-time basis. Cumberland Posey dealt with that by insisting his players behave impeccably and always look as if they were heading to church. The *Kansas City Call* stated that the Monarchs

acted so courteously they could be mistaken for a proper English family.

The owners possessed a deeper reason for these high standards as well. In segregated America, successful black athletes shone as blacks who, even amidst discrimination, could rise to the top. Their stories gave hope to millions of other African Americans that they, too, could succeed in their given fields. In 1940 few blacks worked in the professional arenas—there were only about four thousand black doctors in the United States, and the number of wealthy black businessmen barely registered against that of white entrepreneurs. Besides ministers and teachers, blacks looked to baseball players as role models.

One of the earliest promoters and players of black baseball stated as much in the early 1900s. Sol White wrote in 1907 of the profound implications baseball could have for improved treatment of African Americans: "Base ball is a legitimate profession. It should be taken seriously by the colored player, as honest effort with his great ability will open an avenue in the near future wherein he may walk hand-in-hand with the opposite race in the greatest of all American games—base ball."[18]

The Negro World Series

The regular season for the Negro league games ended in September, when the leaders of the two divisions, the National League and the Eastern Colored League or its later replacement, the Negro American League, squared off in the Negro World Series. Because of the uncertain economic situation, some years featured only enough teams for one division, thereby eliminating the World Series.

In all, eleven Negro World Series were held from 1924 through the late 1940s. In the initial contest, the Kansas City Monarchs defeated

One of the most popular players in the history of the Negro leagues, Leroy "Satchel" Paige prepares to throw a fastball during a 1941 practice.

Hilldale, five games to four, but failed to draw significant crowds. The total attendance for ten games (one ended in a tie) was only 45,857, with the deciding contest drawing a mere 1,549 fans. In regular season games, the Monarchs typically drew 10,000 fans for Sunday double-headers, but oversaturation from a combination of league play, an attractive all-star game that started in the 1930s, and barnstorming games diminished the appeal of a World Series that never seemed to catch on with the fans in the same fashion as the white World Series did in the major leagues.

Even the players did not consider the Negro World Series a premiere attraction. They certainly shrugged off the paltry pay which, in 1925,

One of the most celebrated teams arose in 1931 when Pittsburgh businessman and racketeer Gus Greenlee started the Pittsburgh Crawfords. Greenlee hoped to emulate other famed squads that came before, such as the Chicago American Giants and the Homestead Grays. Instead of a Pullman car, his players rode in a sleek bus bearing the team name, "PITTSBURGH CRAWFORDS BASEBALL CLUB," on its side. He eventually collected so many top stars that other players called the Crawfords "the Yankees of Negro baseball." Five future Hall of Famers, including Satchel Paige, Josh Gibson, Cool Papa Bell, Oscar Charleston, and Judy Johnson, performed for the Crawfords.

Unlike some owners, who delegated administrative details to subordinates, Greenlee took an active interest in his club. He often could be found at the bus's steering wheel, cigar in mouth, driving his team to the next stop. When he was not involved in team matters, Greenlee supervised his two other Pittsburgh businesses —the Crawford Grille, a popular restaurant, and the illegal numbers betting racket.

In the depths of the Great Depression, Greenlee accumulated enough money to build his own stadium, the six thousand seat Greenlee Field. Few teams in the Negro leagues enjoyed a home stadium, but Greenlee wanted his players to have the best.

Greenlee gave the best, but he expected the same in return. Their superb play established the Crawfords as the team to emulate in the 1930s.

Often considered the greatest black baseball team of all time, the Pittsburgh Crawfords pose in front of their team bus in 1935.

handed each man on the champion Hilldale team about eighty dollars, while the losing Monarchs took home fifty-eight dollars. A reporter for the *Chicago Defender* accurately reflected the common sentiment when he wrote in 1926 that "the ballplayers would rather barnstorm against the big-leaguers or other league clubs than to win a league championship to enter a world series as handled the past three years." [19]

As much as league play provided stability to Negro baseball, the real money and the more dramatic pairings unfolded in the other realms—barnstorming tours around the United States and playing overseas during the winter months. Athletes refined their skills, earned extra money, and showcased Negro talent to fans living in regions that could not afford to maintain league teams.

The Great Barnstorming Tours

League play provided structure to black baseball, but not its special identity. Barnstorming—bringing top-quality baseball to hundreds of towns, large and small, rural and urban—did that. A unique culture evolved around the games that distinguished black baseball from the white major leagues.

Hoopla and Heroics

"I shall never forget the first time I saw Rube Foster," gushed player David Malarcher of the legendary Rube Foster and his American Giants when they arrived in New Orleans during Malarcher's grade school years. "I never saw such a well-equipped ball club in my whole life. I was astounded. Every day they came out in a different set of beautiful uniforms, all kinds of bats and balls, all the best equipment."[20]

It is not surprising that Malarcher was so interested in the team's equipment, for the future star took the technical aspects of the game seriously. Most fans, however, turned out for the fanfare as well as the superb play. A combination of hoopla and heroics drew them to the ballparks by the thousands.

"We'd come to a town in our Model-T Ford and go up and down the street with a megaphone—didn't have microphones then— and say, 'Come out to the ball park,'" explained Chet Brewer, who pitched for six different teams between 1925 and 1948. "It was the only way we knew how to get the people to come. Didn't make much money, but we had a lot of

fun playing, because we loved the game."[21]

Before the advent of television or the Internet, which today instantaneously spread news of events, promoters adopted different strategies. Many towns, eagerly awaiting the day the black ball club arrived, hosted huge parades to advertise the coming contest. Bands, local musicians, and veterans' units marched through the streets, basking in the cheers that welcomed the ballplayers who accompanied the parade, resplendent in their uniforms. Usually, one of the town's men with a booming voice broadcast information about the ball game through a bullhorn, while young boys and animals sprinted at the edges of the foray. "Now how many people can hear a bullhorn, a small brass band, howling boys, and barking dogs and not stop what they're doing to see what the fuss is about?"[22] asked Frazier Robinson, a catcher in the 1940s.

Barnstorming Begins

Barnstorming occurred as early as the late 1880s, when the Cuban Giants headed to Florida after their New York resort closed for the winter. In the Sunshine State, the Giants staged contests for hotel guests. From that humble start, barnstorming teams continued to offer a premium attraction well into the 1940s.

Barnstorming could be highly profitable for the top squads. Very few cities in the United States boasted a major league franchise until

Started in 1911 by acclaimed pitcher Rube Foster, the Chicago American Giants boasted one of the most powerful lineups in black ball. At one time or another, John Henry Lloyd, Smokey Joe Williams, and Oscar Charleston played for the Giants.

Foster, along with his white business partner John Schorling, made sure his team had the best, including five different sets of uniforms, a full stock of equipment, and a luxurious Pullman car. Foster added a grandstand holding nine thousand seats to a rented Chicago park to accommodate the throngs who wanted to watch his spectacular team. Foster loved to dazzle his opponents with blinding speed on the base paths and a talent for utilizing the bunt.

In the days before the Negro leagues existed, Foster brought black baseball to many parts of the United States. He arranged tours throughout Canada, and south to California and Florida during the winter resort season.

Foster's experience in running the Chicago American Giants handed him the necessary talents for organization. He later put that effort into starting the Negro National League in 1920.

The 1919 Chicago American Giants pose with their owner, Andrew "Rube" Foster (back row, wearing suit).

The high cost of travel kept most baseball fans from attending games featuring stars such as New York Yankee Babe Ruth (far right) and the other members of Murderer's Row.

expansion in the 1960s, which meant that only a small percentage of the population ever saw quality baseball. The high costs of travel prohibited most fans, black or white, from heading to large cities like Chicago or New York to watch a major league game. Barnstorming offered an attractive alternative. Instead of the fans traveling to where baseball was played, black barnstorming teams brought baseball to the fans. Most people still might never enjoy the chance to watch the New York Yankees and the famed Babe Ruth and Murderers' Row, but now they could at least sit back and pass a pleasant summer afternoon watching baseball showcasing men who knew how to play the game.

Barnstorming teams developed unofficial circuits in which they returned to the same cities each year around the same time. The Kansas City Monarchs monopolized the Midwest and Great Plains regions with a series of talented squads. Exciting, top-caliber play unfolded to baseball-starved fans, who madly cheered for their hometown squads in the delirious hope that they might defeat the visiting professionals.

Barnstorming provided other, less noticeable benefits for the players. The athletes intermingled with white culture far more than they normally would have, which helped both groups better understand one another. In some

Barnstorming teams offered entertainment and fun to thousands of baseball fans around the country. The average citizen in the first half of the twentieth century never had the chance to watch a major league ball game in person, but he could enjoy the competition provided by black barnstormers. In his 1995 book *A Complete History of the Negro Leagues*, Mark Ribowsky quotes a Pittsburg, Kansas, newspaper account that summarized the arrival of a team:

"Today the town is in ferment. Broadway, the main street, streams with traffic, all bound north to the fairgrounds. The Fords and Essexes, the Chevies and Darts, the Buicks and Hupmobiles growl along, bumper to bumper, many rural communities, small white boys might hesitantly walk up to touch one of the black stars, for many had never before seen a man of color. On the other hand, the players gained the praise of white audiences, who applauded their athletic prowess.

bearing Missouri, Oklahoma, or Arkansas tags. The players had dressed a block down the street at the Y with its showers and lockers, essential for all the fried chicken, hams, piccalilli, cakes, pies, and other edibles the townsmen will present through the day to the Monarchs.

"At the fairgrounds, scores of little boys and girls stand shyly on the plot of grass where the bus unloads. Each one [of the players] goes marching off toward the field with this little girl carrying his sunglasses, this small Negro boy with his baseball shoes, these blond brothers with his two bats, this barefooted Italian lad with his glove. Frank Duncan resembles a Pied Piper, since it requires a small battalion to carry his vast array of catching equipment."

"We'd Play Every Day"

Since baseball has long been a popular activity in the United States, the barnstorming teams experienced little difficulty arranging matches. Hundreds of towns had teams featuring the area's top players, all jumping at the chance to show they could compete against the big-name black stars. Various industries supported company teams, while semipro leagues and colleges offered additional competition. Sculling Steel Mill in St. Louis and the Chicago Post Office, for instance, acquired a reputation for fielding great teams.

With such an abundance of opportunities, barnstorming occurred almost year-round. During the regular league season, black athletes might participate in a league game early in the afternoon, then join a barnstorming team for a second contest in the twilight. "We were always booked somewhere every day," stated Buck Leonard of his play in the 1930s and 1940s. "There never came a day when we weren't booked to play a game somewhere. Never. Out of those 17 years we didn't miss but two ball games, and both of them were during the war [World War II] when gas was rationed and we missed our train connections. We'd play every day." [23]

Two games in one day became the norm for barnstorming, and some teams even faced tripleheaders on festive occasions such as July 4. Players suited up for a 10:00 A.M. start in one town, raced to a nearby city for an early afternoon appearance, then sped to a third for a late-afternoon match.

Even poor weather did not deter the barnstorming teams from taking the field, for a canceled game meant no paycheck. The game had to go on, despite nasty conditions that would mean cancellation in the major leagues. A late 1930s incident illustrates this. Gene Benson was traveling with his teammates in a bus toward Cleveland, Ohio, when a car smacked into the bus and flipped it over. Two people riding in the car died in the crash, while the team bus, now a mangled heap, lay smoldering on the roadside. Players emerged with broken ribs and lacerations. "We called the owner," recalled Benson. "He asked how many were dead. We told him no one was dead. The next thing he said was, 'Play the ball game'—they had 8–9,000 people in the stands. I had stitches in my leg and ran them out playing the double header."[24]

A Bit of Entertainment

Barnstorming added a feature that fans would never see in the more serious league play—comedic antics that delighted spectators, even when the actions sometimes bordered on the ridiculous. In hopes of attracting larger crowds and in an effort to avoid embarrassing the usually outclassed opposition, the athletes put on a show for the fans. In the more relaxed atmosphere that surrounded these contests, they could showcase their skills in ways they would never think of doing during the season.

Some players warmed up with routines similar to those that later caught on with basketball's famed Harlem Globetrotters, in which infielders pretended to toss about an imaginary baseball or threw balls behind their backs. An outfielder might take a newspaper onto the field and act like he was reading it during the action, all the while watching play through a small hole he had cut into it so that he could catch any fly ball hit his way. Oscar Charleston and Martin Dihigo, two of black baseball's greats, sometimes played all nine positions, and acclaimed Olympic track star Jesse Owens sometimes staged running exhibitions before a contest.

One of the most popular and talented opposing teams that accompanied black squads in their tours, the House of David from Benton Harbor, Michigan, featured players from

Martin Dihigo sometimes played all nine field positions during barnstorming games as a way to entertain the fans.

a Jewish religious community with bushy beards and flowing hair that reached to the middle of their backs.

Pepper Bassett earned the nickname "the Rocking Chair Catcher" in the 1930s because he sat in a rocking chair behind home plate. This antic drew even the most bigoted white fans. One man in Texas boasted to his buddies that "I didn't care if I was the only white man in the stands, I was gonna see that nigger in the rocking chair."[25]

The bounds of entertainment could be stretched to the absurd. One team played in drag and entered towns billed as an all-female squad. J.L. Wilkinson touted his All Nations team, an assortment that included whites, blacks, Cubans, Native Americans, and a woman he called Carrie Nation.

Clowning

The most outlandish—and, to some observers, offensive—behavior came when teams inserted ethnic stereotypes in their routines, especially those publicized by white promoters such as Abe Saperstein and Syd Pollock. The Zulu Cannibals and the Ethiopian Clowns boasted players named King Tut, Wahoo, Tarzan, and Monkey, who painted their faces, donned wigs and grass skirts, and headed barefoot onto the field. Kansas City Monarch first baseman Buck O'Neil said of a team called the Zulu Giants, "These were the guys that played in straw dresses and wore makeup like we'd see in the Tarzan movies; they would paint their faces like they had a ring in their nose; a lot of them wore wigs, but they wore baseball shoes and socks."[26]

This reliance upon racial stereotypes, which appeared throughout the long history of black baseball, did not sit well with everyone. The editors of the *Indianapolis Freeman*, a black-owned newspaper, wrote on January 27, 1917,

The white man now, and has in the past secured grounds and induced some one in the role of the good old Nigger to gather a lot of athletes and then used circus methods to drag a bunch of our best citizens out, only to undergo humiliation, with all kinds of indignities flaunted in their faces, while he sits back and grows rich off a percentage of the proceeds.[27]

Other black publications labeled this type of entertainment as demeaning to blacks and condemned them as dangerous steps reinforcing age-old stereotypes depicting blacks as shiftless, happy men with toothy grins. Wendell Davis, a sportswriter for the *Pittsburgh Courier*, wrote, "Negroes must realize the danger in insisting that ballplayers paint their faces and go through minstrel show revues before each ballgame. Every Negro in public life stands for something more than the role he is playing. Every Negro in the theatrical and sports world is somewhat of an ambassador for the Negro race—whether he likes it or not."[28]

Many of the athletes agreed and refused to participate. Gene Benson, who starred in the 1930s and 1940s, explained, "There was no foolishness, no clowning. Some of us were approached [to clown], but we all turned it down. We were ball players, we had some principles. We weren't clown ball players; we played *baseball*."[29]

"After All, We Were Pros"

League play never saw the clowning of barnstorming games, and even in barnstorming, the level of lighthearted play varied according to the caliber of the talent arrayed against them. The worst thing a traveling squad could do was embarrass the local nine by horsing around too much and still handily defeating them, which

Negro leagues players wear grass skirts, wigs, and face paint during a barnstorming tour. Such racial stereotyping drew criticism from both the media and the players.

all but precluded an invitation to return the following year. Usually a team would arrive in town, and if they knew nothing about their opponent, they would talk to the residents to learn how skilled was their opposition.

"After all, we were pros and the other teams were fellows who were playing once a weekend," said Arthur W. Hardy, who played in Kansas from 1906 to 1912. "So Topeka Jack [a fellow player] would always talk to the local people. He'd say, 'Now what about you folks here? Do you want us to put on some funny kinds of acts? Or do you think they [the local team] would resent it?'"[30] They might ask the umpire to favor the home squad in any close calls. On the other hand, if the home team was amenable, they might run the bases backward

or bat on the opposite side of the plate. Only one thing would cause a team of black athletes to purposely humiliate the opposition—racial taunts. The opponent could mutter derogatory comments about their skill or their uniforms, but racial epithets drew a speedy and harsh response.

On occasion, the opponent proved formidable. Sometimes two black teams from the Negro league arranged a tour and played each other before different crowds, or one team challenged all-star squads compiled from the white major league rosters. One group even arranged games against Buck Weaver and Swede Risberg, two implicated members of the infamous 1919 Chicago Black Sox team that purposely threw the World Series.

The Great Barnstorming Tours **37**

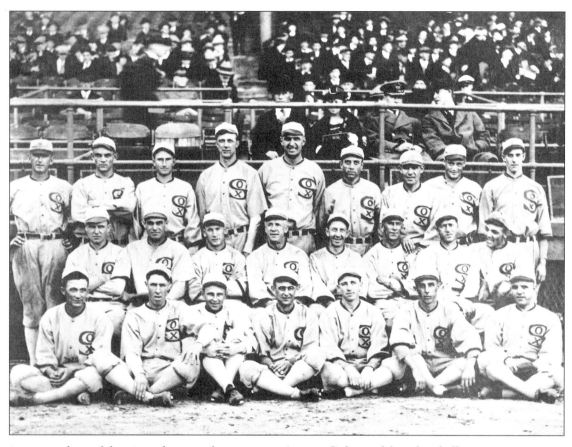

Some members of the 1919 Chicago White Sox team (pictured), banned from baseball for fixing the World Series that year, played in Negro leagues barnstorming games.

"Man, You're Spent"

Amid all the turmoil of a multicity barnstorming tour, one fact was certain—no one could predict the condition of the field on which the game would be played. Unless they rented a big-league stadium, which was usually reserved for Negro league play on the weekends, players became accustomed to rocky infields and outfields hacked out of a pasture. The speedy outfielder Cool Papa Bell, considered one of the greatest players in Negro league history, so badly skinned his legs from sliding on rough terrain that he taped sponges to his sores to prevent further injury.

Games became harder to play, but more popular for the fans, when J.L. Wilkinson constructed the first portable lighting system in baseball so the athletes could perform at night, when more fans had finished their day's work and could attend. The lights, which ran on gas, emitted excessive noise and smoke, and since the illumination provided was poor compared to the modern lighting systems that today adorn ballparks, fielders and batters followed the ball's flight with great difficulty.

Desperate measures had to be taken. In some contests, both sides agreed that a hitter would receive a double for any fly ball hit too high for the outfielders to see. Instead of using fingers to relay signals to the pitcher, which could not be readily seen through the haze, catchers sent signals with their gloves. Some towns erected a white canvas fence along the outfield to aid the batter in picking up the ball.

The arduous schedule took a toll on even the best-conditioned men. Lacking the skilled trainers employed by modern teams, the athletes taped themselves for games, gave each other back or arm rubs, and treated their own cuts and bruises. Since teams carried at most only fifteen players, few men left the lineup with nagging injuries or when in slumps, even if it meant they had to play three games in one day. Pitchers Smokey Joe Williams and Dick Redding provide an example that occurred with regularity in barnstorming. In the early 1920s they faced each other in a doubleheader. Redding defeated Williams in the first game, 1–0, then Williams outperformed Redding in the second and bested him by the same 1–0 score. Each man tossed eighteen innings in one day.

"You were tired," explained Buck Leonard:

You'd ridden 200 miles to get there, rode all night last night maybe, you're going to play here today, and you got a game to play tonight somewhere. You've got to change your sweatshirt after this game, go some-where maybe 50 miles to play tonight; you're trying to save a little from this evening's game for tonight's game. Man, you're spent when you played a double-header at Bushwick or Yankee Stadium or the Polo Grounds. Then you go out there at night to play, you're stiff, tired and you're just forcing yourself.[31]

Travel

The games provided afternoons and evenings of fun, but the athletes paid a high price in the seemingly endless hours traveling to each city. While their major league counterparts traveled by train, Negro league players had to sit for hours in cramped buses and other means of transportation. A few of the top-notch clubs, benefiting from better financing and organization, traveled by train, but most spent so much time in buses or antiquated automobiles that they thought of them as home.

"We used to ride three or four nights in that big bus and never see a bed," said Chet Brewer, who played from 1925 to 1948:

Portable Lights

The introduction of portable lights by J.L. Wilkinson increased attendance at games and widened the popularity of black baseball, an especially crucial point considering that in the 1930s much of the nation was battling an economic depression. While the device aided the game, not all players reserved praise for lights. In addition to hitting and fielding in inferior lighting, the teams had to play more games. In his book *Black Diamonds: Life in the Negro Leagues from the Men Who Lived It*, John Holway includes a quote from Jake Stephens about the effect of the new lighting:

"When they put those lights in and you played a doubleheader in the afternoon and a night game some other place, that's when they [the owners] made sure they made money. Play a doubleheader Saturday afternoon, play a night game Saturday night, and a doubleheader Sunday, then go to Freeport or some other place—six games in two days."

We'd play in one town at night and then after the game, shower in the shower room, get in that bus, ride all night to the next town and get out and go to some little hamburger joint and have some lunch, go to the ball park early, wash our underwear out, hang it up to dry, wash our socks and things. Then when the game was over, we were clean. We lived out of our shaving kits with toothpaste and what-have-you.[32]

In one five-month stretch in 1932, the Pittsburgh Crawfords traveled seventeen thousand miles throughout the South to play ninety-four games. Willie Wells, a member of the Homestead Grays, recalled playing one game in Pittsburgh, Pennsylvania, on Friday, another the next day in Toronto, Ontario, Canada, and a third on Sunday in Detroit, Michigan.

"On Sunday in Philadelphia we'd go to the YMCA at five o'clock in the morning to change clothes," recalled Jack Marshall, who played in the 1920s:

We'd get into uniform and go up into Jersey and play a game at nine o'clock for some picnic or something. We'd leave from there and go to Dexter Park in Brooklyn and play the Bushwicks a doubleheader, and leave there and go out on Long Island and play a night game. It would be five o'clock the next morning when we'd get back to Philadelphia.[33]

The roads traveled were nothing like the modern interstate highways, replete with miles of smooth concrete and dotted with rest stations. Bumpy, dusty, single-lane country roads tested the limits of each ballplayer, already weary from playing one or more games and twisting his back to relieve the discomfort caused by the hard wooden bus benches.

"I've ridden in a wagon fifteen or twenty miles and then slept all night in a railroad station to catch a train to get into the next place," explained Arthur Hardy:

We used to carry our clothes in a roll, and whenever we got caught out, like in a railroad station or someplace, we'd unroll that for a pallet to sleep on, you see. We tried to book games all along the railroads. But sometimes, here off maybe twenty-five or thirty miles, was a little town with a team that had a tremendous following, and we would make that town. We'd have to make it by any transportation we could get. Sometimes we'd have delivery rigs; other times we'd have a hay wagon or just a plain dray with boards across it to sit on.[34]

A Tough Road Ahead

George Giles, a member of the Homestead Grays, rode in what he and his teammates called the "Hotel Buicks," vehicles barely large enough to squeeze in nine men. They packed only a toothbrush for the longer trips and learned to sleep by leaning on each other's shoulders.

"You show me a ballplayer in our old league," reminisced Cool Papa Bell, "and I'll show you a guy that can sleep standing, sitting, or walking. We didn't know how bad it was until some of our guys got into organized baseball. Then we could compare things."[35]

Without the existence of fast food restaurant chains that populate today's highways, and with many places closing their doors to blacks in the segregated society of the early 1900s, the players could not count on locating a decent place to eat while on the road. To tide them over, they brought cold cuts, sardines,

A white man and a black man drink from segregated fountains in the South. America's segregated society made life difficult for many Negro leagues players on the road.

cans of beans, crackers, cheese, lemonade, peanuts, and other snacks they could eat while riding on the bus.

"Everyone had his box lunch under his seat," remembered Wilmer Fields. "Bread, baloney, ham, tomatoes, sandwich spread, and a knife. We called it our 'frigidaire.'"[36]

To pass the time on their frequent road trips, some of the athletes formed singing groups that belted out barbershop tunes or solemnly recited Negro spirituals. Others played cards or chatted, and at least one team member sat with the bus driver to ensure that fatigue did not cause an accident.

If a team decided to sleep in a hotel, it usually had to select a lesser establishment rather than an exclusive hotel due to lack of money and to segregation. Men slept two or three to

a bed to reduce costs, and others combated critters in the night.

"Sometimes we'd stay in hotels that had so many bedbugs you had to put a newspaper down between the mattress and the sheets," said Leonard. "Other times we'd rent rooms in the YMCA, or we'd go to a hotel and rent three rooms. That way you got the use of the bath, by renting three rooms. All the ballplayers would change clothes in those three rooms, go to the ball park and play a doubleheader—nine innings the first game, seven innings the second game."[37]

Love of the Game

Despite the harsh conditions, few players complained. They enjoyed a vastly superior lifestyle compared to the alternatives—drudgery in a coal mine or laboring in dusty farming fields—and they knew that hundreds of other black athletes would gladly trade places with them. Players took the games—especially league contests—so seriously that they often stayed up late at night discussing their errors or ways to approach different teams. "When we lost a game we'd sit up practically all night discussing it," said Ted Page. "Why did we do that? This is the way I had to keep from washing windows in a downtown store or sweeping the floor. Well, if you're gonna play on these teams, you got to win."[38]

They also played for love of the game. According to Ted Page, Josh Gibson played a twilight game in Pittsburgh one night, drove 600 miles to St. Louis for an afternoon game the next day, then drove another 350 miles to Kansas City to play a doubleheader in 110-degree heat. That night, Page watched in astonishment as Gibson, after playing four games and driving 950 miles in three days, joined a group of kids he spotted playing a friendly game of pickup.

"When you're doin' something you love to do, there's nothin' lousy 'bout it," said Jimmie Crutchfield, who played from 1930 to 1945. "And, to me, I thought it was the first step toward the top of the world, man."[39]

Pay

An informal pay structure existed in the barnstorming teams that traveled around the country. In the absence of legally binding contracts, players readily switched teams whenever the incentive proved alluring. A man might suit up for one team on Monday, then appear for another on Tuesday.

Agents who arranged the games usually received 10 percent to 40 percent of the gate,

with the remaining money going to the teams. One reason that barnstorming teams kept the number of players to a minimum was so they would not have to divide the pot among too many players. At times, teams passed a hat among the spectators in hopes of boosting the

Negro leagues great Josh Gibson once drove 950 miles in three days to play games in three different cities.

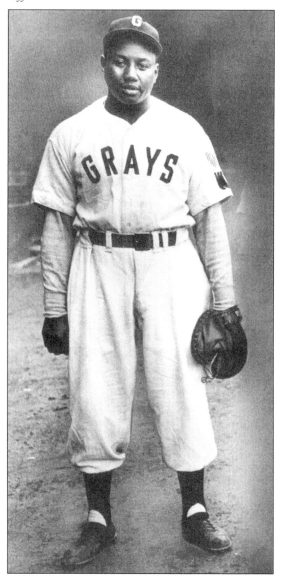

take. In the 1930s, the average Negro leagues player earned $500 a month during the baseball season. The average white player in the major leagues earned $1000 a month.

After the Game

Once their game for the day had ended, the athletes occupied the rest of the time in various ways. Players might spend time strolling in parks, idly chatting on the porches of hotels, or earning additional money singing for traveling salesmen.

In the larger cities, such as New York and Chicago, they could attend the numerous nightclubs that catered to African Americans, such as New York's Cotton Club or the Apollo Theater. Stars in their own domain, the ballplayers mingled with heralded talents from entertainment, such as singer Nat King Cole, musicians Count Basie and Duke Ellington, comedian Redd Foxx, and famed tap dancer Bill "Mr. Bojangles" Robinson. Along with the handful of black physicians and other black professionals, the ballplayers and entertainment stars received the adulation of many and enjoyed a status that few could attain.

League play and barnstorming comprised a large portion of a ballplayer's professional life. Once the season ended, however, their careers did not halt. Other places beckoned for the black athlete.

"I Am a Man"

Like their cohorts in the white major leagues, some ballplayers in black baseball headed home to jobs outside baseball once the league season ended, for unlike today, most players' salaries would not cover an entire year's expenses. Many entered factory work and others labored in the fields. For a large group, though, baseball happily turned into a twelve-month occupation. Once they finished their league play and the barnstorming tours, those athletes headed to distant climes, where a much friendlier reception awaited them.

Florida and California Winter Ball

As soon as the Negro league season wound up with the World Series in September, many players joined winter ball clubs located in Florida and California. They did so for two reasons— they loved playing the game, and they needed the money. "None of us made enough that we didn't have to work in the winter, not even Satchel Paige,"[40] explained Buck Leonard.

Groups of ballplayers first traveled to Florida where, like their predecessors, the Cuban Giants, they performed for tourists who flocked to warmer temperatures in the winter months. Frequently, noted resorts would hire entire Negro league teams to spend the winter months in Florida. Rube Foster's Chicago American Giants, for instance, forged a relationship with the Royal Poinciana Hotel in Mi-

ami. The resort paid the men to play for their customers, and also offered jobs as bellhops or waiters at the hotel or in town to supplement their salaries.

A handful of players drove to Florida on their own and signed to play with one of the local independent teams. The Jacksonville Red Caps added Negro league players on a regular basis.

The California Winter League, organized by California resort owners in an attempt to draw tourists from the wintry east, also beckoned. The league was hugely popular with baseball fans along the West Coast in the 1930s and 1940s, since California boasted no white major league franchise. California baseball offered a mixture of black stars, white professionals, local talent, and Mexican ballplayers. Occasionally, as in Florida, a wealthy California businessman arranged for an entire team to play in return for a percentage of the gate.

The black ballplayers participated in a series of contests up and down the coast, although many games occurred in the main centers of population, such as Los Angeles. Fans hopped into their cars and headed to Wrigley Field in Los Angeles to spend a relaxing winter day in the sun watching great talent play a game they could otherwise see only by traveling back east. Sometimes the games pitted black all-stars against a white major league all-star team. Cleveland Indians pitcher Bob Feller and St. Louis hurler Dizzy Dean were two who organized groups of their fellow major leaguers to play in these games.

"A Sense of Freedom"

As important as winter ball in the United States was to the athletes, nations to the north and south provided an arena offering more attractive benefits. Canada, Mexico, Cuba, Venezuela, and other countries eagerly sought the best players, no matter what their skin color.

The black ballplayers, accustomed to tempering their behavior to the whims of a segregated United States, thought they had entered a paradise. Fans wildly cheered their exploits on the field, followed them with adulation off the field, and hailed them as heroes. Newspapers printed articles recounting their feats. This reception happened back home, but only among

St. Louis Cardinals pitcher Dizzy Dean helped organize teams of major league players to compete against Negro leagues players.

the black population. In Cuba and the Dominican Republic, the welcome came from all segments of society. The men could enter any restaurant, stay in the best hotels, and forget that in the United States they had to accept second-rate status.

In the 1930s, for instance, a Negro league player averaged about five hundred dollars per month during the regular season. In Latin America, he could expect anywhere from six hundred dollars to four thousand dollars a month, a luxurious apartment, and his travel

Many black players like Ray Dandridge earned money by playing baseball in countries like Mexico and Cuba.

expenses covered by the team. The Cienfuegos team near Havana, Cuba, gave each player a residence in the wealthiest section of town, complete with kitchen, dining room, study, living room, balcony, two bedrooms, and a maid. "I told one of the white major-leaguers that this had to be just as good as the majors and he laughed at me," related Max Manning, who played in Cuba. "He said this was better than the major leagues."[41]

The athletes felt they had entered a different realm, one in which skin color mattered little, and they reacted with enthusiasm. "It was a sense of freedom," said Bill Cash, who played in Cuba. "You would be real thirsty and see a water fountain and look above it for the White Only sign and there was none. Water never tasted so good. Your team, all black guys, would stay in Havana's best hotel. You could go wherever you wanted and take your wife wherever you wanted. It was wonderful."[42]

Cracks in the Wall

The men played one game each day instead of the multiple daily contests they would play back home, they rarely had to endure lengthy bus or train rides, and they played on integrated teams. The Mexican league played only three games each week, usually in beautiful stadiums equipped with the finest seating and locker room accommodations. Teams generally offered laundry service and a shoeshine boy.

When some white ballplayers first arrived in Cuba, Mexico, or one of the other Latin American countries, they objected upon discovering they would play alongside black athletes. Team management quickly handled these complaints. It informed them they would either accept the situation as it was and join their black teammates, or they could purchase the next plane or boat ticket back to the United States.

Most whites, however, reacted like Carl Erskine of the Brooklyn Dodgers. The great pitcher freely offered advice on how to play the game to his black teammates in Latin America. Max Manning struggled with his changeup pitch until Erskine showed him how to fake a fastball and deliver the changeup with the same motion.

These interchanges, while small in number compared to the antagonistic events blacks faced in the United States, created a few cracks in the wall of segregation. White players observed blacks firsthand, instead of picking up their information about their talents secondhand. They realized these athletes could play, and above all, that these players were men, not inferior humans. "I think it helped the players get to know one another," said Monte Irvin. "We respected them and they respected us."[43]

Willie Wells found a home in Latin America. He drove to Mexico one winter and so readily adapted to the pleasant environment that he quit the Newark Eagles and remained to play summer ball as well. "Not only do I get more money playing here, but I live like a king," said Wells. "I've found freedom and democracy here, something I never found in the United States. I was branded a Negro in the States and had to act accordingly. Everything I did, including playing ball, was regulated by my color. Well, here in Mexico I am a man. I can go as far in baseball as I am capable of going."[44]

Cuban Paradise

Cuba was the first nation outside the United States to attract black ball players to winter ball. Starting in 1907, each year from December until April Cuba hosted a winter league

Playing baseball in Latin America meant much more than an extra paycheck for the black athletes. For the first time, they experienced what it felt like to be treated as men, instead of second-class citizens. In his book *Voices from the Negro Leagues,* Brent Kelley includes the following quote from Max Manning, the great pitcher in the 1930s and 1940s, about his time in Latin America:

"I'll tell you. You know how it is when the sun comes up after night? That's pretty much what it was like. I'm saying in terms of being somebody, when you went to Latin America, you were somebody and you were treated as somebody and the newspapers treated you as somebody and the people treated you as somebody.

"One of the things I think that did drive the black ballplayers was that they all wanted to go through that window and get down there because everybody would come back talking about it, so you played harder in order to get there. You had a goal that you wanted to achieve: to get to Latin America."

Famed Negro leagues pitcher Max Manning enjoyed playing in Latin American countries, where segregation did not exist.

that drew top talent from all over North America and Latin America. The ballplayers loved Cuba because of its proximity to home and because it possessed such rabid fans. For the first time the players saw a glimmer of what it must be like for the great white athletes back home, such as Babe Ruth and Ty Cobb, for in Havana a crowd of forty thousand was the norm rather than the exception. "They were fanatics," stated shortstop Dick Seay, who played twenty-two years for eight teams in the United States. "They'd throw oranges or lemons at us depending on whether they liked us or disliked us."[45]

Latin Americans had other ways of showing their approval, much to the delight of the black ballplayers. If a man hit a game-winning home run, fans stuffed dollar bills through the wire-mesh fence in appreciation. Wilmer Fields once collected nearly two hundred dollars after smacking a winning round-tripper.

Black players also warmed to Cuban ball because it offered them a chance to compete with white athletes on a daily basis. A man could earn his way into the starting lineup regardless of his color. In the United States, top-caliber black ballplayers had to endure the indignity of watching less talented white athletes bask in the major leagues while they toiled in the segregated black leagues. In Cuba and elsewhere, where only talent counted, a black player had the chance to prove he could match or top the best offered by his white counterparts.

Once he made the squad, the black athlete then had the opportunity to see how he measured against famous white ball players from the United States and determine if he possessed the talent to compete in the white major leagues. Each winter season, future Hall of Fame white players headed south to earn additional money, which meant that a renowned player like John Henry Lloyd could pit his skills against Ty Cobb, Tris Speaker, and, in some years, even the mighty Babe Ruth.

The easygoing schedule in Cuba appealed to every man. Rather than enduring grinding doubleheaders or playing six games in four days, ballplayers in Cuba played a game on Thursday nights and a doubleheader on Sundays.

"Didn't Matter What Color You Were"

Latin America provided many other places to play ball besides Cuba. Puerto Rico and the Dominican Republic hosted vibrant leagues in the 1930s, while Panama, Mexico, and Venezuela followed suit in the 1940s.

A handful of adjustments, although posing minimal problems, caused some discomfort for the athletes. Players fell ill from drinking unsafe water, and others struggled with the language differences and often-dangerous treks along narrow mountain roads. Outfielders in sweltering Venezuela could feel the heat through their shoes, so they learned to constantly shuffle their feet to avoid burns. These concerns, though, paled in comparison to the benefits.

"Not only do I get more money playing here, I am not faced with the racial problem," explained Willie Wells. "When I travel with Vera Cruz [Mexico] we live in the best hotels, we eat in the best restaurants and can go anyplace we care to. I've found freedom and democracy here."[46]

In an effort to monopolize Mexican baseball and field an unbeatable team, Mexican millionaire Jorge Pasquel mounted a major drive to import the best black ballplayers. Pasquel insisted that his players live in the best conditions, inhabit the finest homes, and dine on the choicest foods. He hired special tutors

A sportswriter once asked Honus Wagner, the superlative shortstop for the Pittsburgh Pirates, who the best player in baseball was. As William Brashler relates in his book *The Story of Negro League Basbeall*, Wagner had no doubt: "If you mean in all baseball, organized or unorganized, the answer would have to be a colored man named John Henry Lloyd." Babe Ruth and others agreed—Lloyd could hit and field with the best.

Born in Palatka, Florida, on April 25, 1884, Lloyd became one of black baseball's first major stars. Like many other boys of his time, he quit elementary school to take a job as a delivery boy and help his parents pay the bills. Every day after work, Lloyd played baseball with a group of buddies from the neighborhood. He developed quickly, and as a teenager joined the Young Receivers, a semipro team in Jacksonville.

From 1905 until 1931, Lloyd played for all the great black teams of the day, including Hilldale, the Chicago American Giants, and the New York Black Yankees. He developed a reputation as a deft batter and gutsy fielder. In one 1920 game against Ty Cobb, who loved to slide into bases with his spikes high, Lloyd wore iron shin guards under his stockings. The first time Cobb slid into second base, he hit those shin guards and bounced away from the base toward the outfield. Lloyd and Cobb played four more games in the series—Cobb never again attempted another steal on the second baseman.

After compiling a career batting average of .342, Lloyd retired in 1932 and worked as a janitor in an Atlanta high school. He died in 1964, twelve years before baseball inducted him into the sport's Hall of Fame.

John Henry Lloyd is remembered as one of the best players in baseball history.

so the men could bring their families along. He offered top salaries to Negro league stars such as Josh Gibson, Monte Irvin, Roy Campanella, and two dozen others. Satchel Paige earned two thousand dollars a month, and Cool Papa Bell and others played for more money than they had ever hoped to earn in the United States.

Bill Cash fondly recalled his Mexican league play, which he compared with any other form of the sport. "The competition was first-rate. You had some very good Mexican players. The fans loved the team, not Mexicans, blacks, or whites, but the team. Didn't matter what color you were—a hit was a hit and they cheered like crazy. I loved it down there and played for three years."[47]

Public praise accompanied the improved pay. The fans loved the sport, which they called *beisbol,* and treated their sports heroes as if they were national treasures. Chet Brewer, who played for two seasons in Panama, could hardly believe the reception he and the other ballplayers received. "The second year we won the Caribbean Series. It's the only time Panama won the tourney. We were the poorest country of all of them. The other players laughed at us when we lined up for the pre-game ceremony. We looked like boys in knickers. But after the victory, there were parades and parties all over Panama City."[48]

"El Presidente Doesn't Lose"

The most unique episode in overseas baseball occurred in the Dominican Republic in 1937. In an effort to gain popularity among his country's baseball-crazed people and to one-up a political rival who fielded a potent team, the nation's dictator, Rafael Trujillo, assembled the mightiest squad that money could buy. Trujillo enticed black baseball's most recog-

In 1937 President Rafael Trujillo of the Dominican Republic recruited Negro leaguers to help his team beat the team of a political rival.

nizable star, Satchel Paige, with six thousand dollars for the six-week season, and provided him a parcel of money with orders to bring other top players with him. Within a few days Paige gave Josh Gibson and Cool Papa Bell three thousand dollars each to play, then signed other stars for lesser amounts.

"He [Trujillo] figured since his people liked baseball so much, if he came up with a top-notch team they wouldn't want to see him lose his job," related Cool Papa Bell. "So he imported a bunch of us from the States. We didn't know we were being used for a political reason until we got there."[49]

That reason delivered quite a surprise to the players, who assumed they could travel to the Dominican Republic, play a handful of games for six weeks, and head back to the United States, richer and happier. It almost turned to tragedy.

Their first indication of turmoil happened immediately after the star-studded team lost a series of games to one of Trujillo's archrivals, a squad of players from Santiago. Bell, Gibson, Paige, and the others returned to their hotel to find a group of soldiers waiting. With menacing looks on their faces, the soldiers pointed their rifles into the air and loosed a volley of shots as an officer warned the Americans, "El Presidente doesn't lose. You know you are playing for El Presidente."[50]

So warned, Paige and his cohorts turned serious. The next time they faced Santiago, they swept the series.

The Game of Their Lives

As the final playoffs neared, Trujillo, concerned that his efforts might fail, posted armed guards around the players' hotel to ensure they focused on the championship series. Escorts headed out with the players whenever they stepped outside to eat or to spend some time at a beach. Nightclubs and other hot spots were declared off-limits. Despite the safety precautions, Tujillo's all-stars split the first six of the seven-game series.

The night before the championship game, the dictator tossed the Americans in jail to keep them from distractions. Instead, the tactic only worried many of the men. When they entered the ballpark the next day, they witnessed a more disturbing spectacle. Soldiers lined both the first- and third-base sidelines, Trujillo's armed men lined up along the first-base stands and his rival's men along the third-base line. The sight made Bell and the others wonder if there would be trouble no matter what the outcome.

The normally placid Paige started the deciding contest, but he found this game to be one of the most difficult of his career. He concluded that if he lost the game, it would most likely mean his death. He wrote in his memoirs, "If we win, their whole army is gonna run out and escort us from the place. If we lose, there is nothin' to do but consider myself and my boys as passed over to Jordan [executed and gone to heaven]."[51] People told Bell he and his teammates would be shot if they failed to win for Trujillo.

The men had faced discrimination all their careers, but this was the first time they played a ball game with their lives on the line. The tension showed, and some of the players committed errors during the course of the game. The outcome seemed in jeopardy as late as the seventh inning, with the Americans trailing 5–4. Fortunately for Paige, Bell, and the others, Trujillo's team rallied to win the championship, 6–5. Rather than remain for the celebration, many of the black stars hurried from the stadium and purchased tickets back to the United States.

"Just Like Heaven"

Latin America was not the only place offering dignity and opportunity to black ballplayers. To the north, Canada opened its arms to men

Born in 1896 in Indianapolis, Indiana, Oscar Charleston used baseball to escape a hard childhood. At age fifteen he ran away from home and entered the service, where he joined his regiment's baseball team while serving in the Philippines.

Charleston joined his first Negro team in 1915, when he signed with the Indianapolis ABCs. He loved to play center field directly behind second base to cut off those soft drives up the middle. If a batter smacked one over his head, Charleston relied on his speed to catch up to the ball.

He was equally as gifted at the plate. Famous hurler Dizzy Dean claimed that he so feared Charleston that whenever he faced him, he just threw his best pitch and hoped Charleston would fail to lock on to it. Charleston hit .434 in 1921, when he led the league in batting average, doubles, triples, home runs, and stolen bases.

By 1923 Charleston was one of the best-paid players in Negro baseball, earning $325 a month, in part because of the fans his name attracted. As Robert W. Peterson notes in his book *Only the Ball Was White*, the *Pittsburgh Courier*'s Chester L. Washington wrote of Charleston, "Scores of school kids turned out regularly just to see Oscar perform. He was to them what Babe Ruth is to kids of a lighter hue."

Charleston's lifetime batting average of .357 stands with the best in the sport. He died in Philadelphia in 1954.

Oscar Charleston, shown here in 1942, was a gifted fielder and hitter, batting .357 over his career.

who, to the immediate south, chafed under severe restrictions.

Catcher Frazier Robinson, who played in Baltimore in the 1940s, could hardly believe the difference when he first traveled to Canada. Instead of being made to feel like a servant, for the first time Robinson understood what it meant to be treated as an equal in a mixed society.

"Off the field, Canada was like no place I'd ever been" he later wrote:

> Never did I imagine such a place even existed. Living and eating conditions were very much nicer. I never ran into a restaurant or a hotel that wouldn't take me. Nothin' up there like that. Canada was like paradise. You could go to any café you wanted. There was nowhere you couldn't go, nowhere you couldn't eat, no nothin' like that. After playing in Texas and Oklahoma and in the south, it was as different as night and day. You went wherever you wanted to go, and nobody bothered you. People didn't even look crossways at you. Even the police didn't bother you. The police up there didn't even have no pistols on them. All they had was sticks. It was just like heaven. [52]

Robinson roomed at a YMCA with fellow players Leon Day and John Britton. The trio experienced a welcome in society that extended from the baseball field. A local rugby team asked Robinson and a group of players to sing a collection of songs to entertain the audience at an important rugby contest.

The caliber of play offered plenty of excitement. Robinson caught one of his most memorable games when his Winnipeg Buffaloes grappled with the Brandon, Manitoba, Greys for the Man-Dak League championship.

Pitcher Leon Day settled into a marathon affair against the Brandon pitcher, finally winning in seventeen innings, 1–0. Robinson caught the entire game, then wobbled off the field on exhausted and rubbery legs.

Wilmer Fields starred for several seasons for Brantford, Ontario. A force on the mound, he also demolished opposing pitchers at the plate, accumulating averages approaching .400 and winning several most valuable player awards. Sam Bankhead moved from managing the Homestead Grays to directing the Farnham, Quebec, squad in the Provincial League. This made Bankhead the first black man to manage a team comprised mainly of white ballplayers.

In the late 1950s, after the Negro leagues had folded for good following Jackie Robinson's demolition of the color barrier, Canadian baseball offered an alternative for black athletes. The Negro leagues had provided a home for those players who did not possess enough talent to join Robinson in the majors, but with its collapse, they had nowhere to turn except to the north. Canada continued to offer jobs that once had been provided by the Negro leagues.

"I have very fond memories of playing in Canada," stated Frazier Robinson. "Both in uniform and out, the Canadians were very good to me. I knew that I was past the age to play [in the U. S. major leagues], and I didn't let that bother me. The only thing I wanted to do was find a place to play until I retired, and I finally found that place in Canada." [53]

Benefits

Despite the occasional hazards and inconveniences, black ballplayers experienced many benefits from playing in other nations. At home, executives and players in the white

Negro leagues player Jackie Robinson (left) and Brooklyn Dodgers general manager Branch Rickey shake hands after Robinson signs his contract in 1948.

major leagues claimed that blacks could not compete at the highest level, but their contributions in Mexico, Cuba, and elsewhere proved otherwise. Some defended the unofficial color line in baseball by stating that blacks and whites could not form a harmonious team, an argument rebutted successfully by the mixed Latin American squads. Others contended that blacks could not handle the so-called skilled positions, such as catcher, where a man has to call a game for the pitchers. Again, white players on Latin American teams saw black athletes capably holding these spots.

These nations also offered a unique world to the black athletes, for here they were judged as men based upon their exploits, not their skin color. As long as they performed to the best of their ability and acted in accordance with the local customs, they received equitable treatment. Latin America became a tropical refuge from the ills of a segregated United States.

Wilmer Fields explained,

Back home we'd want to dine out, so we'd find a black-only restaurant. Down there [Latin America] we'd just walk into any restaurant we'd want. There'd be black Cubans at tables next to us, black Americans on the other side, some white tourists behind us. Nobody down there thought this was a big deal. Me, I was shocked. Very pleasantly shocked. I think that's the big reason all of the guys would go down there to play, to get away from all the segregation crap. [54]

Their play in Latin America thus punched holes in many of the arguments that buttressed segregation's insidious system. Blacks and whites could play baseball together, could compete on an even basis, and could treat each other with respect. The black players required every weapon in their arsenal, however, for they again faced bitter times in the United States once they returned home.

4 "Black in a White World"

The fair treatment encountered by black ballplayers when they traveled to other nations lasted only as long as the baseball season there. If they wanted to return to the land of their birth, as 99 percent did, the players would once more live in a system that placed obstacles in their paths and constantly reminded them that, because of their skin color, they occupied an inferior position. Segregation smacked the black player twice—it forced him to compete in a separate league, and it subjected him to further abuse while playing within that league. On and off the field, athletes faced the sting of bigotry.

Jim Crow

The roots of unfair treatment stretched back into the depths of slavery and the resulting hatred that accompanied the freeing of the slaves following the U.S. Civil War of 1861–1865. In 1828 a white minstrel show performer, Thomas Dartmouth Rice, created a popular routine called "Jump Jim Crow." Because he blackened his face, the name "Jim Crow" gradually became associated with phrases, actions, and laws that restricted black freedoms, especially a series of laws passed by the Southern states after the Civil War. Jim Crow laws, such as those forbidding blacks to drink at white water fountains, to eat in white restaurants, or to sit wherever they wanted on public buses, gradually removed access to many of society's amenities for black men and women.

These odious practices reached into baseball, the sport so many people loved to call America's pastime. In 1884, when Moses Fleetwood Walker wanted to play in an American Association game for his Toledo team against a squad from Richmond, Virginia, someone dispatched a letter protesting the use of the black star:

> We the undersigned do hereby warn you not to put up Walker, the Negro catcher, the evenings that you play in Richmond, as we could mention the names of 75 determined men who have sworn to mob Walker if he comes on the ground in a suit. We hope you will listen to our words of warning, so that there will be no trouble; but if you do not there certainly will be. We only write this to prevent much bloodshed, as you alone can prevent.[55]

Four names appeared at the letter's end, but when a Richmond reporter scoured the town's records, he could find no evidence of people with those names. The issue became moot when Walker had to sit out with a broken rib, but the letter's ominous tone showed that some Americans were far from ready to accord decent treatment to blacks trying to participate in a sport with whites.

Three years later Doug Crothers, a white player, refused to sit for a team picture because he would have to appear with blacks, something

Thomas Dartmouth Rice performs his "Jump Jim Crow" routine in this painting. The phrase "Jim Crow" became associated with laws that restricted black freedoms.

he felt his Southern heritage would not permit. As he tried to explain in an interview,

> I don't know as people in the North can appreciate my feelings on the subject. I am a Southerner by birth, and I tell you I would have my heart cut out before I would consent to have my picture [taken with blacks]. I could tell you a very sad story of injuries done my family, but it is a personal history. My father would have kicked me out of the house had I allowed my picture to be taken.[56]

Insults and Humiliation

In 1888 the *Indianapolis Freeman* newspaper reported that after the most famous black team of the day, the Cuban Giants, defeated the white champion squad from New York, other white teams from St. Louis, Chicago, and Detroit refused to play them. Rather than be beaten by black athletes, the three teams preferred to shun them.

Frazier Robinson listened in astonishment in 1936 when a white umpire announced over the public address system the lineups for that day's barnstorming game in Hobbs, New Mexico. The man casually used words that would incite hostile reactions in more civilized times, but the slurs simply reflected the state of mind in the 1930s. "Today's the day of the big ball-game," blurted the announcer. "For the white boys, it's Ted Blankenship pitching and Beans Minor catching. And for the niggers, it's a big nigger pitching and a little nigger catching."[57]

Chet Brewer heard all kinds of insults from the fans during his time with the Kansas City Monarchs. Spectators shouted derogatory

"So Far Shall I Go"

Segregation in baseball had pernicious effects on the black player who was excluded. Possibly the most harmful was what segregation did to the man's future. In one of the earliest books printed about black baseball, *History of Colored Base Ball,* Sol White discusses this issue:

"When he [the black ballplayer] looks into the future he sees no place for him on the Chicago Americans or Nationals, nor the Athletics, or New York, even were he superior to Lajoie, or Wagner, Wadell or Mathewson, Kling or Schrock. Consequently, he loses interest. He knows that, so far shall I go, and no farther, and, as it is with the profession, so it is with his ability."

Sol White (back row, middle) poses with his Philadelphia Giants teammates and coaches.

comments, and, as Brewer recalled, many white fans had trouble determining who was who. "All of us [the pitchers on KC Monarchs] were tall and black, and we were all throwing hard," said Brewer. "The fans would say, 'Which one of them niggers was Satchel?' They didn't know Satchel from the rest of us. It was awful the way the white people talked about us. We entertained them and beat the socks off them. We'd ignore their insults and just beat the pants off them."[58]

Some Support

Some institutions supported the black athlete. As early as 1889 the *Sporting News* listed some of the ways blacks had been mistreated in baseball: white ballplayers purposely shunning black teammates, coaches signaling improper instructions to make black players look bad, and white pitchers throwing at their heads. The publication concluded sympathetically, "Race prejudice exists in professional baseball ranks to a

Satchel Paige waits in the Kansas City Monarchs' dugout. Paige, like most Negro leagues players, was often forced to contend with the racist attitudes of white fans.

marked degree, and the unfortunate son of Africa who makes his living as a member of a team of white professionals has a rocky road to travel."[59]

White ballplayers sometimes came to the defense of black players, but before the 1920s they tended to either keep silent or offer lukewarm support. "While I myself am prejudiced against playing in a team with a colored player," stated one ballplayer in 1889, "still I could not help pitying some of the poor black fellows that played in the International league."[60]

After the 1920s the bitter feelings among players subsided to a degree, but by then the only white athletes who competed with blacks did so voluntarily on barnstorming tours. More and more, the black athlete gained acceptance from white players. His problems intensified, however, when he stepped off the field and reentered normal society.

"Roll with the Punches"

From traveling arrangements to food, housing to clean clothes, athletes who played in the Negro leagues or barnstormed realized they could never have what they wanted. Babe Ruth and Lou Gehrig enjoyed their choice of exquisite hotels and five-star restaurants, but blacks had to be content with establishments that catered to them. The players accepted it, although grudgingly. "Having a hard time finding a place to eat or sleep may not seem like a big deal until you've played a couple of ballgames, been stuck for a couple of hours in a hot bus, and are tired and hungry,"[61] explained Frazier Robinson of the trying conditions.

Players might spot a sign that said "Wel-Kome to Klan Kountry" in a Southern state, referring to the white supremacist group the Ku Klux Klan, or be forced to remain belowdecks on a ferry along with the cars and cargo, while whites roamed about on the open deck above. Conditions improved to a degree in the Northern states and the Midwest, but even in those friendlier regions, black ballplayers faced hostility.

"Abilene [Kansas]! Never will forget it," exclaimed George Giles, who played from 1927 to 1938:

> Went out to play an exhibition game, and I never heard the expression nigger used so much in my life. It was "nigger this" and "nigger that," and "look at that nigger run." I told the manager, "Man, let's hurry up and get this game over with so we can get out of town, 'cause I'm tired of hearing this word nigger." But it was just one of those things you learn to accept. You just roll with the punches. That was the way it was all over the country. See, we played all the states. Colorado was just as bad as Mississippi. New York was just as bad as Alabama. It was all the same.[62]

"I Never Could Understand This Racial Thing"

Sleeping arrangements could be excruciating. After traveling on a hot bus for hours on end, the athletes pulled into their next stop, weary and hungry. Before settling down, they had to locate an establishment that would house them, and another to feed them. Sometimes, the same people who the next afternoon would cheer their exploits on the baseball field now refused to serve them food.

Players used a variety of methods to handle the problem. The Kansas City Monarchs set up a network of boardinghouses around the country that would accept black customers. Some teams slept in tents set up in fields and

The Ku Klux Klan, a white supremacist organization, sometimes made traveling through the South difficult for Negro leagues players.

shared food with homeless people during the Depression, or roomed with black families that graciously opened their homes to the travelers. Other times, in the larger cities that offered more possibilities and a large local black population, the team checked into one of the second-rate hotels that welcomed blacks.

Gus Greenlee usually provided the best for his teams, but even he could not always guarantee his players the finest accommodations. Denied shower facilities in an Ohio ballpark, the players once had to accept an offer from a local woman and share a tub of water. In many locations Greenlee, knowing the trouble they

would experience finding a good restaurant, had the bus pull over at fruit and vegetable stands so his athletes could purchase food.

"We couldn't stay in white hotels, we couldn't eat in restaurants," explained George Giles:

In cities there were usually Negro hotels. In those small towns we would stay in family houses, two players here, two players there. Sometimes they'd fix us a meal in the colored church, or we'd bring out food from the grocery store in a paper sack. If we were in Nebraska, we'd ride all night to Lincoln or Omaha. In some of those small towns we couldn't stay, and sometimes we'd just ride all night and sleep in the bus. Then we'd have to play ball the next day. A lot of times we couldn't take a bath after the ball game. I remember once in Colby, Kansas we set tubs of water out in the sun to get them warm so we could take a bath.[63]

Denied permission to eat in an Alabama diner, Monte Irvin and a group of players asked if they could at least drink from a well around back. The woman grudgingly gave her approval. After the team had quenched their thirst, Irvin watched the woman pick up the water scoop they had used and smash it to bits.

"I never could understand this racial thing," said George Giles of the antagonistic atmosphere in which he had to perform. "It was kind of disgusting. When we were barnstorming, the white teams would stay in a hotel, and we'd be changing clothes in a farmer's barn. We've been in towns where they wouldn't even sell us sandwiches to take out."[64]

Baseball Resistance

Censure from officials in the white major leagues nudged black ballplayers farther from equal treatment. In the early years of the twentieth century, white teams sought contests with the best black squads, especially during World War I when attendance lagged. Gradually, though, some white owners refused to play black teams, mainly to avoid what they considered the embarrassment of white players losing to their black opponents. Brooklyn Dodgers owner Charles Ebbets fined his star pitcher, Rube Marquard, for participating in a game against black athletes after the 1917 season. Ebbets explained his reasoning when the press quizzed him about the fine:

> The Brooklyn team is averse to permitting its team, or any of its players, participating in games with Negroes. There are only semiprofessional Negro teams, and when there is an outcome like yesterday's game, when Rube [Marquard] was beaten, President Ebbets believes it tends to lower the caliber of ball played by the big leagues in

"Terrible with a Capital T"

Ask a ballplayer from the Negro leagues about his experiences, and inevitably he will mention some aspect of segregation. Most do not refer to it with bitterness; they only include the reference as part of the story. Mahlon Ducket, who played in the 1940s, shared this account with author Brent Kelley, who included it in his book *Voices from the Negro Leagues*:

"[Traveling through the South was] terrible. Terrible with a capital T. It was a problem for me at first because I was born and raised in Philadelphia and we had a little segregation here but nothing like they had down there in the '40s. In the '40s it was terrible. They had the [Ku Klux] Klan down there, they had lynchin's and so forth. That was the only thing—my mother, she was a little leery. She was always afraid when we went below Washington [DC]. Well, I had to do it, you know, when we went to places like Alabama and Mississippi, Louisiana, and so forth."

the eyes of the public, and at the same time make the major league team the subject of ridicule at the hands of the more caustic fans.[65]

When Judge Kenesaw Mountain Landis became commissioner of the major leagues in 1920 he quickly, but quietly, instituted a ban on white teams competing against black players. He contended that baseball suffered whenever a major league team lost to a black team, and he ordered that if any major leaguer barnstormed with blacks, he could not wear his official team uniform.

"Race Was Always Something You Were Aware Of"

Even the strongest of individuals would have trouble living and working under the miserably poor conditions faced by black baseball players. In early childhood, they became aware that they had to accept their status as second-class citizens in segregated America. Now, though they had proven with their skills that they belonged on the same field as white ballplayers, they still could not join the major leagues. They could do little, though, except swallow their pride, push negative thoughts out of their mind, and hope one day the white major leagues would open the door.

"Race was always something you were aware of," said Frazier Robinson, "and it seemed like just when you'd pushed it to the back of your mind, you'd see or hear something to remind you that you were black in a white world."[66]

Blacks who grew up in Northern states reacted astonishingly when they saw firsthand what segregation in the South meant to their fellow blacks from that region. Some had never heard the word "nigger" until they played in the South, and others had difficulty accepting that black adults in the South had to call even white teenagers "Mister."

At least one athlete was overwhelmed by segregation. In 1912

Famed major league pitcher Rube Marquard was fined for playing in a 1917 Negro leagues game.

In 1920 baseball commissioner Judge Kenesaw Mountain Landis (shown here opening the 1928 World Series) banned all major league teams from competing with black players.

Luis Bustamente, a talented dark-skinned Cuban, agonized over his exclusion from the major leagues because of his skin color. He chafed at reading about less-talented white players gaining glory in the majors while he had to play in a separate league. Bustamente could not quietly go along with the inequality and drank himself to death. In a suicide note, he explained why: "I'll drink until I become stupefied. Thus, I will eliminate myself [from baseball] as useless, keeping deep within me the conviction of what I am worth but what they won't let me prove simply because I have had the immense misfortune of being a Negro."[67]

The bitter atmosphere caused most black athletes to suppress their hostile feelings and focus on their sport. They felt they could accomplish little to improve the situation, anyway, at least until the white baseball world

In the days when the major leagues banned black ballplayers, many black fans followed the majors. They read of their exploits and opened their wallets to purchase tickets and hot dogs. As Jules Tygiel includes in his book, *Past Time: Baseball as History,* noted black newspaper reporter Wendell Smith had this to say about the situation in 1938:

"Why we continue to flock to major league ball parks, spending our hard earned dough, screaming and hollering, stamping our feet and clapping our hands, begging and pleading for some white batter to knock some white pitcher's ears off, almost having fits if the home team loses and crying for joy when they win, is a ques-

tion that will probably never be settled satisfactorily. What in the world are we thinking about anyway?

The fact that major league baseball refuses to admit Negro players within its folds makes the question just that much more perplexing. Surely, it's sufficient reason for us to quit spending our money and time in their ball parks. Major league baseball does not want us. It never has. Still we continue to help support this institution that places a bold "Not Welcome" sign over its thriving portal and refuse to patronize the very place [Negro leagues baseball] that has shown that it is more than welcome to have us. We black folks are a strange tribe!"

opened its gates to them. Most players assumed this was a long time coming.

"All We Ask Is to Be Treated Fairly"

In halting steps over the years, a handful of organizations resisted segregation in baseball. Walter S. Brown, a black businessman in Baltimore who served as president of the National Colored League, said in 1887, "All we ask is to be treated fairly and given only half a chance and we will prove to the public that colored men are great ball players and give satisfaction to the entire public."[68]

In 1912 the *St. Louis Post-Dispatch,* one of the most influential white-owned publications in the nation, wrote of the predicament facing organized baseball and issued what, for those times, was an amazing statement in support of the black athlete: "[We wonder] if baseball is, after all, the great American

game. We play it, to be sure, but the colored people play it so much better that the time is apparently coming when it shall be known as the great African game."[69] While this was hard for many whites to read and was, in some ways, an overstatement, it helped some people grasp the harm of two separate baseball worlds.

The *Newark Call,* a black newspaper, published persuasive arguments why the inequality should end:

If anywhere in this world the social barriers are broken down it is on the ball field. There many men of low birth and poor breeding are the idols of the rich and cultured: the best man is he who plays best. Even men of churlish dispositions and coarse hues are tolerated on the field. In view of these facts the objection to colored men is ridiculous. If social distinctions are to be made, half the players in the country will be shut out. Better make character and personal habits the test. Weed out the toughs and intemperate men first, and then it may be in order to draw the color line.[70]

With their actions on the field, black ballplayers emphasized the assertion that on a level playing field, whether inside or outside baseball, blacks could compete with whites. They also altered the notion of some white fans that blacks were inferior. From that humble beginning, it was but another leap for people to believe that blacks could also compete in business, medicine, teaching, and other professions. Black baseball's most enduring legacy may have been this effect.

Black baseball was a showcase of skill in every contest. However, two major arenas offered an extra measure of excitement and talent—all-star games during league play and barnstorming contests against all-white squads. In both, they proved that the black athlete deserved notice.

"They Knew There'd Be a Good Show"

While most black baseball players performed in front of small crowds in run-down stadiums, every so often they enjoyed the limelight. The East-West Negro League All-Star Game attracted huge throngs and created thrills that other games lacked. Exhibitions against white all-star teams provided the opportunity to match talent with the major leaguers. These games brought wide acclaim to black baseball and gradually gained the attention of white owners, who realized that a lucrative market existed in the black population.

"A Joyful Experience"

The most publicized spectacle of Negro baseball started in 1933 when business executives Roy Sparrow and Gus Greenlee arranged for a game to be played in Chicago's Comiskey Park, the home of the white major league White Sox, pitting the best stars from each division in the Negro leagues. Called the East-West Negro League All-Star Game, the game's participants were selected by fans, who cast their votes with either of the two major black newspapers, the *Chicago Defender* and the *Pittsburgh Courier*.

The affair quickly became the most popular event in black baseball. Players felt honored to be chosen by the people, and fans—at least those fortunate enough to be able to travel to Chicago and purchase a ticket—finally had a chance to see the greatest assemblage of talent in the league. The contest even drew a decent crowd of white newspaper reporters and white spectators.

A festive air surrounded the affair. Players arrived and checked into the Grand Hotel, then joined the throngs that packed Chicago's nightclubs to listen to the music of Count Basie, Ella Fitzgerald, and the other entertainment figures who scheduled Chicago appearances to coincide with the game. Monte Irvin, who played in several of the all-star contests, claimed no player enjoyed much sleep because of the activities:

> The East-West Games were a joyful experience. They put red, white, and blue banners up all over the park, and a jazz band would play between innings. People would come from all over the country to be part of this spectacle. The games were good. The players were great. If you could have picked one all-star team from the two squads, it surely could have rivaled any white major league all-star team of the time. That team would have been as good as any all-star team that's ever played. [71]

Between 1938 and 1947 the East-West game outdrew the white major league all-star contest five times. In 1943 more than fifty-one thousand fans packed the stadium for the East-West contest, while the major league all-star game attracted fewer than thirty thousand. The Union Pacific railroad added extra cars to handle the influx of people heading to Chicago for the clash.

"Pandemonium Reigned"

The main benefit of the game was that it brought widespread attention to the top black athletes. The black community knew of Satchel Paige, Josh Gibson, and Cool Papa Bell, but outside of a few rabid baseball fans and sportswriters, the white community remained ignorant of their exploits. This contest placed their names front and center, not only for white fans but for the flock of white major league scouts who attended.

"Those days during the war [World War II] Negro baseball was drawing more fans than it ever did," wrote Satchel Paige in his autobiography. "Everybody had money and everybody was looking around for entertainment and they found plenty in Negro baseball. Even the white folks was coming out big. They'd heard about me and about Josh Gibson and about guys like us and they knew there'd be a good show whenever we were out there."[72]

The 1935 game, which offered Paige as the main draw, exemplified the excitement that engulfed Comiskey Park whenever the East-West contest occurred. "Pandemonium reigned in the West's cheering section," wrote a reporter for the *Pittsburgh Courier*. "An instant later, a hush fell upon the crowd as the mighty Satchell Paige, prize 'money' pitcher of the East, leisurely ambled across the field toward the pitcher's box. It was a dramatic moment. Displaying his picturesque double windup and nonchalant manner, Satchell started shooting 'em across the plate."[73]

The 1948 Negro leagues East All-Star squad poses for a team portrait. The East-West All-Star games brought notoriety to the best black baseball players.

The next year's game topped Paige's antics, offered a thrilling spectacle for fans, and showed why the game had so much entertainment value. Led by Gibson's four hits, athletes from both teams smacked the ball all over Comiskey Park. The game entered the tenth inning tied at 4–4, when the East pushed across four runs.

The West came right back in its half of the inning to knot the score, setting up the dramatics for the eleventh inning. Martin Dihigo, the stellar pitcher from Cuba who played for the New York Cubans, faced slugger Mule Suttles with two men on and two out. With a one ball, one strike count, Dihigo fired a fastball at Suttles,

Ted Radcliff tags out Josh Gibson during a 1944 East-West All-Star game. All-star matchups were often the Negro leagues' most competitive games.

who rocketed the ball toward the outfield fence. Bell and Gibson raced around the bases as the outfielder sped toward the long fly ball, which headed toward the deepest part of the park 450 feet away, a section that only grudgingly gave home runs. The outfielder watched haplessly as Suttles's mighty drive cleared the fence, winning the exciting battle and bringing the fans to their feet in a prolonged ovation.

The East-West game took on significance far greater than its entertainment value. The white press increased its coverage of the black stars, and the major leagues, realizing that sooner or later the color barrier would come down, started to seriously follow the careers of a handful of black talent. Black club owners received a hefty financial contribution from the well-attended event, which helped them keep their clubs afloat and provide opportunities for budding black stars.

The game diverted little extra money toward the players, but they did not mind. The adulation and notice sufficed, and if that did not, the memories did. Monte Irvin claimed that he and the other players usually spent their all-star stipend in one night, but the memories of participating in such a momentous occasion lasted the rest of their lives.

Games Against Major Leaguers

The East-West game brought notice to black ballplayers, but critics of the quality exhibited by black baseball could still point to the fact that African Americans comprised both squads. According to those naysayers, an immense gulf existed that separated play in the white and black leagues.

A partial answer came in the series of barnstorming games through the years between squads of black ballplayers and white ballplayers. At least in these contests one could com-pare the abilities of black athletes with their white opposition.

Before 1924, black all-star teams had the opportunity to play against entire white major league teams. The players looked at these games as chances to prove they belonged in the major leagues from which they were excluded. Though some of the white opponents did not take these games as seriously, since they were exhibition games occurring after the season for extra money, black athletes still received a glimpse of how they could perform against the men they read about in the sports pages.

In 1910 an all-star squad played twelve games in Havana, Cuba, against the Detroit Tigers, which featured future Hall of Famer Ty Cobb. The Tigers won the series, 7–4–1, with Cobb hitting a superlative .371 and teammate Sam Crawford batting .360 for the games. Those averages, however, were fourth and fifth place. The top three hitters—John Henry Lloyd at .500, Grant Johnson at .412, and Bruce Petway at .390—were African Americans.

Five years later pitcher Smokey Joe Williams led his Lincoln Giants to a 1–0 shutout victory over the Philadelphia Phillies, fresh off their World Series appearance. In a tense ninth-inning standoff, Williams struck out the side to wrap up the victory after the Phillies loaded the bases with none out. That same year, major league teams played eight exhibition games against black teams, gaining no more than a 4–4 split against what black baseball's detractors called inferior talent. Given the opportunity, black athletes proved their mettle.

In the 1920s famed white hurler Grover Cleveland Alexander organized white barnstorming teams and set up an exhibition schedule against the top black talent. Dizzy Dean, who won thirty games for the St. Louis Cardinals in 1934, did the same the following decade. The pattern remained the same—black all-star teams generally held their own against white

Grover Cleveland Alexander watches Satchel Paige pitch. In the 1920s Alexander organized white barnstorming teams that challenged the top black squads.

squads, thereby gaining the respect of the white stars.

The Hilldale team played as a unit during one six-game series in 1920. The exhibition proved remarkable in that none other than the immortal Babe Ruth, who had just walloped fifty-four home runs for his New York Yankees, participated. Hilldale captured only one of the six contests, but Ruth and the other players walked away with a higher regard for their black brethren.

After the 1934 season Dean set up an exhibition series against a black all-star squad headed by Paige and Gibson. Dean, who later said that he made more money playing in these games than he did in winning the World Series, paid Paige and the other black stars as much as twelve hundred dollars for two weeks of work.

Skill appreciates skill, so few white players taunted Paige. Chicago Cub Frank Demaree stepped across the line, though, by criticizing the hurler and boasting he had faced far tougher pitchers. Ever the showman, Paige took advantage of the hand-delivered opportunity to upstage Demaree. In an exhibition game, when Demaree stepped to the plate the first time, Paige shouted for his seven fielders to leave the diamond, all but daring the Cub to get his bat on one of his famed fastballs. With only the catcher, Demaree, and the umpires remaining, Paige struck out his adversary in three straight pitches.

"Big League Style"

Gripping contests such as these drew throngs of black and white fans to the ballparks well into the 1940s. J.L. Wilkinson arranged an October 1941 duel pitting black baseball's most publicized team, the Kansas City Monarchs, against the major league's fastest hurler, Cleveland Indian Bob Feller. The game was played in St. Louis's Sportsman Park, a stadium that featured segregated seating—blacks had to sit in the more distant bleacher section in deep centerfield or in a pavilion—and the owners altered their policy when demand for tickets swamped stadium offices. To accommodate the increased requests for tickets from African Americans, the owners announced that blacks could sit anywhere in the ballpark. In its small way, the exhibition game removed another small obstacle separating white and black.

The next year the Monarchs shifted to Chicago's Wrigley Field for a contest against the Dizzy Dean All-Stars. In this game, the first in which blacks played in Wrigley Field, Paige defeated Dean's squad, 3–1. Frank A. Young, sports editor of the *Defender,* praised the teams for drawing a huge crowd of blacks and whites and asserted that the game

proved once and for all that America's baseball fandom want to see a ball game

Black Against White

One of the benefits of white all-star teams barnstorming against black squads was that each side obtained a glimpse of the other side's talent level and an evaluation of their own. Each side could see how well they performed in competition with the other.

Usually, observers used these games to evaluate the skill level of the Negro ball players. Stanley Glenn, who played for the Philadelphia Stars, thought it was the other way around. Bruce Chadwick includes the following quote by Glenn in his book *When the Game Was Black and White:*

"The black players will tell you those games proved how good the blacks were. I say it proved to the white players how good *they*

were. A star in the majors might hit .330 for the season and play a twelve-game barnstorming tour against black players. On that tour, against top black pitchers, he might hit .250. He's going to say to himself, perhaps I wouldn't have that high average if I had to hit these guys all the time. A guy like Jimmy Foxx or Lou Gehrig would hit just as well against us as against the whites, so he knew, and everybody in the country knew, that he was a good ballplayer. We kind of proved things. The major leaguers appreciated where on the spectrum they were and where we were. I think that talk is talk, but when guys, black and white, mix it up on the field a lot—and there were hundreds of these games—then everybody knows who's good and who's not so good."

regardless of race, color or creed of the performers. And while the White Sox were taking a 14-9 licking at Comiskey Park, here was Satchel Paige, Hilton Smith and the Monarchs performing in big league style but denied the right to play in the big leagues because of their color. [74]

Young added that, if anything, instead of preferring major league contests over Negro league baseball, black fans were tired of paying top dollar to watch what they thought was inferior talent while better players languished in the Negro leagues, forbidden to enter the majors by the all-white policy.

"They Never Heard Such a Thing"

A Paige all-star team versus Feller's all-stars in 1946 drew more fans than that year's World Series. The squads played thirty-two games in twenty-six days, and again underscored the point that black ballplayers deserved their places alongside the white major league players.

When Stan Musial of the St. Louis Cardinals earned ten thousand dollars, more than double his recent World Series share, he and others saw the economic impact that black fans asserted and concluded it could only be a matter of time before the major leagues opened their doors to black players. Verdell Mathis recalled of Musial, "He made more money in the first night in Wrigley Field, Los Angeles, than he made in the World Series. Start Musial came to me that night and said, 'You know what? I should have been out here all the time.'" [75]

The white players noticed something else. According to Satchel Paige, they were amazed that the black athletes endured such rough conditions while on the road:

The big leaguers that started barnstormin' with us, they couldn't understand it to save their life. They would have to go in cars. They been layin' up in their feather beds, trainin', and when they began to ride those cars and keep up with us playin' ball, they couldn't do it. They wanted to know how in the world we did it so long. Can't stretch your legs out in four or five hours. They never heard such a thing. [76]

"They Won Some and We Won Some"

The black ballplayers learned from these contests as well. They competed against some of the most heralded players in the major leagues—men like Dizzy Dean, Babe Ruth, Lou Gehrig, and Bob Feller—and found that their skills held up. Few games ended in blowouts; most came down to the final few innings in which a single player smacked a timely hit or snared a wicked line drive. The white major leaguers had more depth on their league teams than the blacks could boast, but in these smaller contests, the black squads matched the whites player for player.

Gene Benson, who played for fourteen years in the Negro leagues, saw little difference: "So as far as the competition, I could see no difference in the major leagues and our leagues, as far as hitting against the different pitchers. When we played head-to-head, it was nip-and-tuck. They won some and we won some. The white ball players knew it. They respected us. They considered us equals." [77]

A white reporter agreed. Shirley Povich, the popular sportswriter for the *Washington*

Major league pitcher Bob Feller (left) talks with Paige. A white all-star team led by Feller played against black all-stars assembled by Paige in 1946.

Post, heaped praise on black players after watching an exhibition game in Florida:

> There's a couple of million dollars' worth of baseball talent on the loose, ready for the big leagues, yet unsigned by any major league. There are pitchers who would win twenty games a season for any big-league club that would offer them contracts, and there are outfielders who could hit .350, infielders who could win recognition as stars, and there's at least one catcher who at this writing is probably superior to Bill Dickey—Josh Gibson. Only

one thing is keeping them out of the big leagues, the pigmentation of their skin. They happen to be colored.[78]

Accurate records were not compiled for every game, since they did not count in any league schedule. As far as can be determined, black squads won about 60 percent of the contests. In the 1920s alone, black teams won seventy-four and lost forty-one against white major leaguers, an impressive record even considering that some white players most likely did not give the effort they would during the regular season, while the black athletes probably played harder because they had a point to prove.

Benefits accrued for blacks throughout the country. First, black citizens gained a sense of achievement in the fact that other black individuals succeeded against the major leaguers. Second, the games provided an afternoon or evening of superb entertainment for fans that normally would not witness a spectacle. Finally, the games demolished the segregationist myth of black inferiority, helped show the folly of segregation, and established the groundwork for a player to come along and smash the color barrier.

The Immortal Paige

Fans of all colors, drawn both by the allure of seeing black against white ballplayers as well as by the prospect of observing top-notch talent, packed baseball stadiums when one of the all-star collections was scheduled for their area. Of the great black stars, three of the biggest attractions, the ones most people paid money to watch, were individuals who stood out for their daring styles and amazing skill: Satchel Paige, Josh Gibson, and Cool Papa Bell. Not only did they bring out the spectators, but at the same time, by proving that the black man could match anything shown by major leaguers on the diamond, they paved the way for Jackie Robinson to come along and open up the majors to African Americans.

The greatest of all, according to most observers, was Satchel Paige. Spectators and fellow players loved watching the youth dazzle opposing batters with his blinding fastball and amazing accuracy. Paige, who loved the limelight, sometimes warmed up by placing a matchbook cover on the ground, then throwing pitch after pitch over it.

Before long, Paige stood out as the main attraction in Negro leagues baseball. He often pitched every day, even if only for a few innings, to satisfy the fans, white and black, that came out to see him.

White America knew his name. Popular national magazines such as *Time, Life,* and the *Saturday Evening Post* printed profiles of Paige in 1940. Ted Shane, in his article for the *Saturday Evening Post,* praised Paige's prowess in words that now would be considered insulting but at the time were viewed as flattery: "Paige, always the showman, would crank his apelike arms a half dozen times, uncrank them, lean back till he almost lay on the ground, bring that huge left foot up till it almost kicked out a cloud, then would suddenly shoot the ball from somewhere out of this one-man melee." Shane quoted rival players as saying, "You cain't see nothin' but dat foot. It hides the ball park and Satch, too! Sometimes you don' know the ball's been pitched till it plunks behind you!"[79]

The top pitcher in the major leagues, Dizzy Dean, handed Paige the highest compliment in 1938 when he told the *Chicago Tribune* that Paige was the greatest pitcher he had ever seen. He said he saw most of the white pitchers people always referred to as greats, such as Christy Mathewson and Grover Cleveland Alexander, "but I know who's the best

Satchel Paige's Rules for Staying Young

The incredible Satchel Paige pitched well past the age most ballplayers remained in the sport. He claimed his secret lay in six rules he followed, although he may have said this with tongue in cheek. Paige listed his six rules in his autobiography, *Maybe I'll Pitch Forever:*

"Avoid fried meats which angry up the blood.

If your stomach disputes you, lie down and pacify it with cool thoughts.

Keep the juices flowing by jangling around gently as you move.

Go very light on the vices, such as carrying on in society.

Avoid running at all times.

And don't look back. Something might be gaining on you."

Satchel Paige gets a rubdown before taking the mound in a 1942 game.

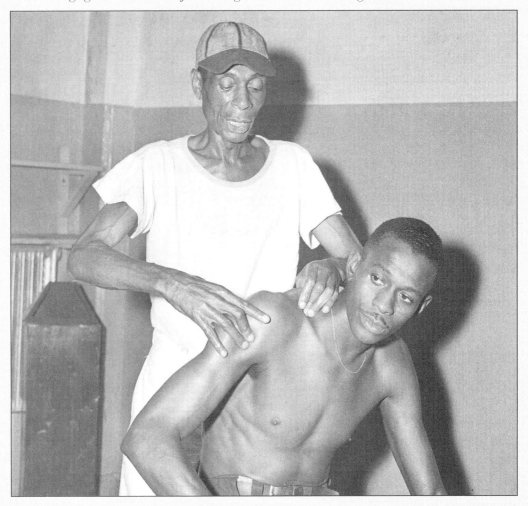

pitcher I ever see and it's old Satchel Paige, that big lanky colored boy. Say, Old Diz is pretty fast, and you know my fast ball looks like a change of pace alongside that little bullet old Satchel shoots up to the plate."[80]

Unreliable records make it difficult to accurately assess Paige's feats. Paige claimed he pitched twenty-six hundred games over his career, including three hundred shutouts and fifty-five no-hitters. Baseball historians place his total wins at around six hundred.

Josh Gibson

When fans hear the name Satchel Paige, they think of strikeouts and showmanship. When they hear the name Josh Gibson, power and home runs flash into their minds. In 1931 Gibson smashed 75 home runs barnstorming through the Midwest, and three years later he recorded another 69. Some historians, hampered by the lack of official records, claim he also once hit 89 home runs in a season, a notable feat even if some came against amateur opposition. In all, historians credit Gibson with smacking 963 home runs in his seventeen-year career, far more than Hank Aaron, Babe Ruth, or any of the other top major league ballplayers, black or white.

"He would have hit more if all the parks had been fenced in like the majors," asserted Cool Papa Bell. "Sometimes the outfielders got back 500 feet and Gibson would still hit the ball over their heads."[81]

Gibson once clubbed a mighty home run in Yankee Stadium, the scene of so many Babe Ruth round-trippers. Gibson's ball smacked just two feet below the top of the stadium wall in center field, 580 feet from home plate, missing going completely out of the park by inches. Observers believed that had the ball been two feet higher and sailed over the wall, it would have traveled 700 feet.

White stars stood in awe of Gibson, who was called the black Babe Ruth. Hall of Fame pitcher Walter Johnson declared, "There is a catcher that any big league club would like to buy for $200,000. His name is Gibson. He can do everything. He hits the ball a mile. Throws like a rifle. Too bad this Gibson is a colored fellow."[82]

"It was just a treat to watch him hit the ball," said Gibson's first manager, Judy Johnson. "There was no effort at all. You see these guys now get up there in the box and they dig and scratch around before they're ready. Gibson would just walk up there, and he would always turn his left sleeve up, and then just before he swung he'd lift that left foot up."[83]

Cool Papa Bell

James Bell epitomized those skills for which neither Satchel Paige nor Josh Gibson were known—knocking out singles and doubles, and speed on the base paths. Nicknamed Cool Papa for the deliberate manner in which the young player once struck out a batter in a tight situation (he occasionally pitched), Bell gained fame for his quickness. Opposing infielders drew closer whenever Bell batted, for they knew if he hit a ground ball to them in their regular, deeper infield position, Bell would beat out the throw. Jimmie Crutchfield claimed that when Bell hit a ground ball back to the pitcher, the other infielders shouted to hurry the throw or Bell would be safe.

"Cool Papa was the fastest man I've ever seen," wrote Buck O'Neil. "But more than that, baserunning isn't only about speed. It's about technique, cutting the corners and keeping your balance. And Cool Papa, he was a master at all of that."[84]

Satchel Paige receives most of the acclaim as the Negro leagues' finest pitcher, but another man ranks close behind. Born in Texas in 1886, Smokey Joe Williams started pitching for the San Antonio Bronchos in 1908. A monster on the mound at six feet, six inches, Williams overpowered hitters with a lightning quick fastball and a devastating drop ball that plunged at the last second.

Williams received his break in 1909 when he pitched against Rube Foster's Leland Giants and struck out nine batters. The young pitcher headed to Chicago, where he began a long career with the Giants and with other top teams, including the Homestead Grays.

Williams dominated the Negro leagues from 1912 to 1923, amassing an incredible 41–3 win-loss record in 1914. As far as can be determined from incomplete records, he often struck out more than twenty players in a game, and once notched twenty-five in 1924. Opposing players marveled at his control and claimed that if Williams walked one man a game the pitcher groused that his control was off. Williams labeled a 1919 contest against Cannonball Dick Redding as his finest game. As John B. Holway relates in his book *Blackball Stars: Negro League Pioneers,* Williams said, "It was a no-hitter. I won it, 1–0. Dick allowed only two singles. I pitched another no-hitter that year against a white team called the Ironsides. In my career, I had five no-hitters."

He performed well against major league opposition as well. He tossed twelve games against major league players, winning six, losing four, and tying two. He gained the attention of the major league players in 1915 when he shut out the National League champion Philadelphia team, 1–0, striking out ten.

Williams retired in 1932. The major leagues honored him with a day in 1950 at New York's Polo Grounds, shortly before he died in February 1951. For his accomplishments, Williams was inducted into baseball's Hall of Fame in 1999.

Smokey Joe Williams pitched five no-hitters during his Negro leagues career.

Bell often scored from second on sacrifice fly balls, raced from first base to third base on bunts, and once scored from second on a ground ball to win the 1934 East-West game. Satchel Paige claimed that Bell was so fast "he could flip the [light] switch and get into bed before the room went dark."[85]

Bell compiled a record year in base thefts by stealing 175 bases in 180 games. In center field, he played so close to second base that fans felt he could never catch balls hit over his head, but he usually did.

Bell played like another fabulous center fielder, Willie Mays. According to Gene Collins,

Center fielder James "Cool Papa" Bell was renowned for his blazing speed around the bases.

a fielder who loved to watch Bell play center field, Bell and Mays "used to turn their back to the infield at the crack of the bat—they'd take one look to see the ball leave the bat, they'd turn their back because they knew the sound of the ball off of the bat."[86]

Paige, Gibson, Bell, and the other players laid the foundation for future black athletes to attain a dream many never reached—competing in the majors. White spectators attended games solely to see them play, which in turn led white club owners to more readily see the profitabil-ity of opening the major leagues. After staring at the forty thousand fans that packed a stadium for one 1939 all-star game, for instance, American League president Will Harridge claimed that the big leagues would be integrated within five years. An integrated major league would have eventually occurred, but through their talent and drawing power in all-star matches, Paige, Gibson, and Bell hastened the process. Diverse factors then came together near midcentury to open the doors to black ballplayers.

CHAPTER 6

"Somebody Has to Make the First Move"

As the 1940s unfolded, the dreams of black athletes to compete in the major leagues were finally fulfilled. The dream opened with a trickle—no mad influx of black stars occurred—but it at least removed the barrier to Negro leagues stars. A combination of black pressure, economic factors, a world war, action by influential whites, and the right man finally opened major league baseball to black ballplayers.

Foundation for Civil Rights

Every athlete who played in black baseball removed a piece of the wall separating white from black ballplayers. Many did not live to see integration, but they proved that black athletes could perform at the same high level as whites. Stars such as Satchel Paige and Josh Gibson, as well as unheralded players such as George Rossiter and Harry Salmon, placed their talent on the field for all to see. The cumulative efforts of hundreds of men, particularly in the famous showdowns between black and white all-star teams, stood as glaring testimony to refute the charge that blacks were inferior to whites.

The Negro leagues offered a chance for blacks to play the popular game, and to become businessmen and learn the intricacies of operating a complex organization. The leagues provided a future at a time when futures seemed dim to most blacks in segregated America, and in doing so offered hope for a better life. In its own way, Negro baseball contributed to the foundation upon which the civil rights movement, with its emphasis on hope, dignity, and opportunity, opened in the 1950s.

Opposition to Integration

Though many observers in the sport recognized that integration was bound to happen, powerful factors still stood in its way. Opponents claimed that major league ballplayers, many of whom came from the South, would never accept playing alongside black athletes, and that white fans would not come to a ballpark where they would have to sit with black fans. "We have always been interested in Negro players but have not used them because of the public," explained Ford Frick, president of the National League, in the early 1940s. "The public has not been educated to the point where they will accept them."[87]

The statement failed to acknowledge that some white players would have accepted integration. They remained silent, however, out of fear of going against fellow teammates or owners or upsetting an institution that had given them a decent living.

Ironically, some team owners from the Negro leagues and the majors opposed integration for the same reason—money. Some black owners worried that if the major league opened their doors to black players, the Negro leagues would no longer have a reason for existing and they would be out of business. At the same time, those white owners who rented their stadiums to black teams were hesitant to lose that source of income, which approached one hundred thousand dollars a year per team.

Kenesaw Mountain Landis, the powerful commissioner of major league baseball, also posed a formidable block to integration. He may have issued public statements subscribing to equal opportunity, but privately he had long been a supporter of separate leagues. A.B. "Happy" Chandler, who became Commissioner after Landis's death, later remarked that as long as Landis remained in office, "there wasn't going to be any black boys in the league."[88]

"The Silly Unwritten Law"

Forces promoting integration slowly gathered steam. Changes in society often occur when those in power perceive an economic advantage in implementing those changes. The success of the East-West game in Chicago, with fifty thousand fans willing to pay good money,

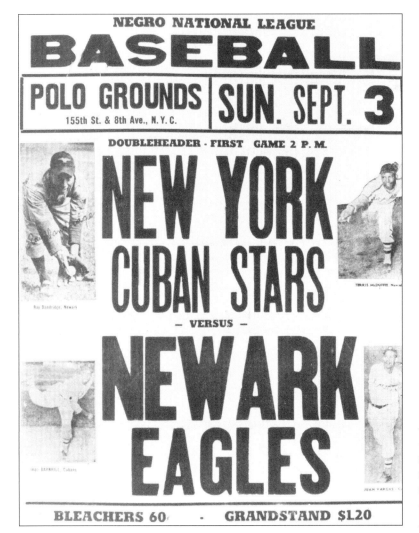

A poster advertises a Negro National League doubleheader. Some black team owners opposed integration, fearing it would result in the collapse of the Negro leagues.

provided such a reason. If black baseball could draw such huge crowds, what might those star players do if they entered the majors?

A group of white sportswriters promoted integration as early as the 1930s. Westbrook Pegler wrote in 1935 of "the silly unwritten law that bars dark Babe Ruths and [Dizzy] Deans from the money they deserve."[89] Other respected white newspaper writers such as Heywood Broun and Shirley Povich also condemned the exclusion of blacks.

A handful of white ballplayers and owners joined in the protests. Pitcher Bob Feller commiserated that black stars had given much to baseball, but that baseball had given little but exclusion in return. In 1937 William

Sportswriter Ford Frick (shown here feeling Babe Ruth's midsection) was an outspoken proponent of integrating major league baseball.

Benswanger, the owner of the Pittsburgh Pirates, then involved in a heated race for the pennant, gushed in a newspaper article how pleasant his team's prospects would be if he could have the likes of Paige, Bell, and Gibson in his lineup: "If [the race question] came to an issue, I'd vote for Negro players. I know there are many problems connected with the question, but after all, somebody has to make the first move."[90]

Many of the black players took a wait-and-see attitude. They knew they could compete in the majors, but segregation had been a fact of life for so long that no one could predict if and when it might end.

Buck Leonard explained this cautious approach:

> I remember we played up to Griffith Stadium [in Washington, DC] one Sunday and a group of black protesters was there. And they came in the clubhouse and said they wanted to talk. They said, "Don't you fellas think you could play in the major leagues?" We said, "Yeah, we think so." They said, "Would you fellas like to play in the major leagues?" "Yeah, we'd like to play in the major leagues," we said. "So why don't you protest or demonstrate?" they said. We said, "You fellas demonstrate and protest, we gonna play. We don't have time." They said, "Well, aren't you part of the movement?" We said, "We're part of the game, not the movement. We're part of baseball."[91]

Leonard added, "We didn't think anything was going to happen. We thought that they were just going to keep talking about it, that's all. They'd talked about it all those years and there'd been nothing done. We just didn't pay it any attention. We'd say, well, if it comes, we hope to have a chance to play, but we just didn't pay it any mind."[92]

World War II Helps

Contributions by African Americans in World War II nudged baseball closer to integration. More than 170,000 blacks served in the military from 1941 to 1945, including many from the Negro leagues. Pitcher Leon Day landed in Normandy only six days after D-Day in June 1944, while Max Manning drove a truck in Europe for the famed supply outfit the Red Ball Express. Monte Irvin, Buck O'Neil, and Lary Doby also served in various capacities.

These men, and the many others who donned uniforms, gave a compelling reason to grant equality to blacks, both inside and outside baseball. How could society ask wartime sacrifices from individuals, then deny them the same basic rights for which they fought and died? "I can play [baseball] in Mexico, but I have to fight for America, where I can't play,"[93] lamented pitcher Nate Moreland.

African American activists rallied behind the slogan "If he's good enough for the Navy, he's good enough for the majors."[94] Pegler compared baseball's treatment of blacks with Hitler's treatment of the Jews in Europe.

At the same time, openings in major league baseball caused by white stars heading overseas did not go to blacks. When Joe DiMaggio, Ted Williams, and Bob Feller left for the service, less talented minor league players, some of whom had failed Army physicals and received medical exemptions from service, took their spots. Joe Nuxhall went directly from his high school baseball team to the majors, and a one-armed outfielder, Pete Gray, started.

Black players joked during the war that if they competed in all-star games against whites, they would be lowering their standards since they still had most of their stars. The humor, though, could not mask the hurt they felt, for baseball had once again passed over black ballplayers. "How do you think I felt when I

The one-armed outfielder Pete Gray played one season in the major leagues in 1945 when many of baseball's stars were overseas fighting in World War II.

saw a one-armed outfielder?"[95] asked a frustrated Chet Brewer.

The men did not realize it, but the collapse of segregated baseball stood just around the corner. The sport needed the right man, the

person who could absorb bigotry on the field and off. Clark Griffith predicted the coming events when he said in an interview, "A lone Negro in the game will face caustic comments. He will be made the target of cruel, filthy epithets. Of course, I know the time will come when the ice will have to be broken. Both by the organized game and by the colored player who is willing to volunteer and thus become a sort of martyr to the cause."[96]

The player would not only open major league baseball to blacks, but help end the long run of Negro league competition.

"We Can't Afford Any Misfits"

Branch Rickey, president of the Brooklyn Dodgers, started the ball rolling by ordering his organization's scouts to scour the Negro leagues, Mexico, and Cuba for the best black star. He wanted an individual who could not only excel on the field, but be a model citizen off the field. Knowing that the first black man in major league baseball would hear innumerable racial slurs, Rickey needed someone who could control his temper. A black newspaper reporter, Sam Lacy, wrote as much in the *Afro-American Newspapers* in 1945: "With us, the first man to break down the bars must be suited in every sense of the word. We can't

afford to have any misfits pioneering for us, and for obvious reasons. Unwilling as they are to employ Negro players, they will be quick to draw the old cry: 'We gave 'em a chance and look what we got.'"[97]

Integration received a boost in 1944 with the death of commissioner Landis. His successor, Happy Chandler, immediately announced that if a black youth could die in Guadalcanal or Italy, he certainly had the right to play major league baseball.

Rickey's scouts gave him Jackie Robinson, a well-known college athlete from California who played in the Negro leagues. Rickey and Robinson met on August 28, 1945, and quickly agreed on a contract. Rickey told the youth he wanted a player who had the guts not to fight when he heard taunts, then handed him a book about Jesus Christ to learn about nonresistance.

The pair announced Robinson's signing and assignment to the Dodger farm club in Montreal on October 23, 1945. Most white-owned newspapers ignored the event, but black newspapers hailed it as an epoch step. The National Association for the Advancement of Colored

"You Always Feel Kind of Quiet"

Satchel Paige never had to serve in the military, but he did his share during World War II by frequently visiting wounded soldiers in stateside hospitals. Paige always experienced the same with each visit—he walked away profoundly moved. He recounts one such occurrence in his autobiography, *Maybe I'll Pitch Forever:*

"I made one of those visits when I was out in San Diego [California]. Somebody told me that some wounded soldiers that'd come home on a hospital ship heard I was in town and wanted to see me. I hurried down to the docks.

I went on the ship and I was so close I could touch them and the doctors told me to go and talk.

Those wounded boys'd lay on their stretchers and say, 'I heard tell of you when I was a baby.' They'd reach out their hands and feel my right arm and'd ask how it hung on there after all those years pitching. White boys and colored boys said it was a long time since they'd seen me and did I still have that fast ball.

You always feel kind of quiet after you leave those boys."

People president Roy Wilkins praised the signing:

The millions who read box scores very likely have never heard of George Washington Carver [an accomplished black scientist], but Jackie Robinson, if he makes the grade, will be doing missionary work with these people that Carver could never do. He will be saying to them that his people should have their rights, should have jobs, decent hours and education, freedom from insult, and equality of opportunity to achieve.[98]

"Cracks in the Wall"

Some of the black players, with a touch of jealousy, remarked that the Negro leagues contained many players who were better athletes than Robinson, and that Rickey signed Robinson only for the money he would bring in at

Albert "Happy" Chandler (throwing ball) integrated major league baseball when he became commissioner in 1944.

Young fans lean over the Brooklyn Dodgers dugout to get Jackie Robinson's autograph. Robinson's participation in the major leagues created opportunities for other black athletes.

the gate. While those comments may have been true, they ignored the fact that with Robinson, Rickey had a player who combined great talent with the right disposition.

"There were players on the Monarchs—such as Bonnie Serrell and Jesse Williams—that, really, Jackie couldn't carry their glove," said Frazier Robinson. "So I think most of us were a little surprised that a more established player wasn't chosen, but we were very happy for Jackie." He added,

When I think back to segregation, I remember a wall. As a black man, I knew that there were places you couldn't go and things you couldn't do. You might look over the wall, but you couldn't get over the wall. And the first cracks I saw in that wall were caused by Jackie Robinson. And from Jackie those cracks in the wall spread throughout baseball. And from baseball to other sports and from sports to hotels and the rest of society.[99]

Jackie Robinson played his first game in a major league organization on April 18, 1946. He collected four hits, including a home run, and stole two bases for Montreal.

The next April, Robinson opened for the Dodgers against the Boston Braves to mark the first appearance of a black athlete in the majors since Moses Fleetwood Walker a half century earlier. Any fears that an African American would frighten away white crowds quickly dissolved; the stadium was packed. Robinson scored a run in the 5–3 Dodger victory, and was named Rookie of the Year for 1947, compiling a .297 batting average, 29 stolen bases, and 125 runs scored in the Dodger's pennant-winning season. For his exploits, *Time* magazine featured Robinson on its September 22, 1947, cover.

Integration of the major leagues came haltingly. In 1948 catcher Roy Campanella joined the Brooklyn Dodgers, and Satchel Paige helped Lary Doby and the Cleveland Indians to a World Series championship by registering a 6–1 record, despite being in the twilight of his career. Their superb play had white fans wondering what other top talents existed in the Negro leagues, and surmising what Paige must have been like in his prime.

Still, progress moved slowly. Not until 1959 did every major league team include a black ballplayer. The measured pace annoyed those stars who believed they could play in the major leagues, but all they could do was sit back and hope their chance arrived before their careers ended.

"Negro Baseball Walked Out"

Ironically, the entry of Jackie Robinson and other black athletes into the major leagues doomed the Negro leagues. Fans who normally spent an afternoon or evening watching a barnstorming team now headed to the nearest major league park, even if they had to travel miles farther, for everyone wanted to see Jackie Robinson. The Monarchs, long considered the top draw in Negro baseball, still had Satchel Paige on its roster in 1947, yet rather than watch the Monarchs play at home, a packed train of Kansas City fans traveled five hours to St. Louis to watch Robinson. The sports pages of black newspapers, long the sturdiest supporters of the Negro leagues, relegated news to the inside while splashing coverage of Robinson on the front pages. Almost every team lost money in 1947 and 1948. "The big league doors suddenly opened one day," wrote Wendell Smith in the *Pittsburgh Courier*, "and when Negro league players walked in, Negro baseball walked out."[100]

In 1948 the Newark Eagles, one of the oldest Negro leagues teams, folded. Its collapse foreshadowed trouble for the Negro leagues, for if such a renowned franchise experienced inescapable financial troubles, the others would likely have difficulties as well. The Negro National League disbanded the same year, two years before the Negro American League folded in 1950.

Black baseball continued to exist into the 1960s, but it barely resembled the glory years. Great players headed to the majors, forcing black teams to rely on second-rate talent or players at the end of their careers. Most teams resorted to clowning antics to draw crowds. A once-proud industry, fashioned in response to segregation, ended when segregation in baseball halted. By giving an arena for black ballplayers to shine, the Negro leagues helped speed their own demise.

"When Jackie Robinson went to the Dodgers, that's what broke up the Negro league," said Dave Barnhill, who played in the 1940s:

They fought so long, so hard to get blacks in the majors. That was a big mistake. The fans followed that one man instead of following the rest of the teams, so the league folded. We pushed to get one up there, should have pushed to get more up there. But we didn't. Just pulled the league down completely. The fans stopped going to the ball games. We had nothing going for us then.[101]

Most did not regret the breakup of their league, for it meant that capable black ballplayers now had the opportunity to perform in the majors. They experienced some regret at never having the chance themselves, but few held on to bitterness. As Frazier Robinson wrote, "I enjoyed my time playing in the Negro leagues and was sorry to see them fold, but if that's what it took to break the color line, then so be it."[102]

The Hall of Fame

As slowly as integration of baseball arrived, it seemed that entry into the Hall of Fame in Cooperstown for Negro leagues players inched even slower. The officials at the hall took little notice of them, and as the years passed, memories of their exploits faded. Older players died or simply disappeared into retirement, while the younger stars grabbed headlines in the majors.

One of the greatest hitters in major league history, Ted Williams, changed that at his induction into the Hall of Fame in 1966. In his acceptance speech, the famous slugger admonished baseball by saying "I hope that someday Satchel Paige and Josh Gibson will be voted into the Hall of Fame as symbols of the great Negro players who are not here only because they were not given a chance to play."[103]

Those comments from such an esteemed ballplayer opened the Hall of Fame. Five years later, Paige was inducted, the first from the Negro leagues to be so honored. He accepted his award with grace, then explained that in black baseball, "there were many Satchels, there were many Joshes."[104] Other men entered the Hall of Fame shortly afterward—Josh Gibson and Buck Leonard in 1972, Monte Irvin in 1973, and Cool Papa Bell in 1974. Baseball had honored thirteen other players by 2001, and a veterans' committee was set up to examine ancient records to guarantee that deserving Negro leagues stars will not be forgotten.

Rookie of the Year

Jackie Robinson had an outstanding first season, despite the tremendous obstacles he faced in being the first black ballplayer in the majors. In naming him Rookie of the Year for his .297 batting average, 29 stolen bases, and 125 runs scored, the *Sporting News* stated that it selected Robinson solely on the basis of what he accomplished on the field. The publication's explanation is included in Robert W. Peterson's excellent volume *Only the Ball Was White:*

"That Jackie Roosevelt Robinson might have had more obstacles than his first year competitors, and that he perhaps had a harder fight to gain even major league recognition, was no concern of this publication. The sociological experiment that Robinson represented, the trail-blazing that he did, the barriers he broke down, did not enter into the decision. He was rated and examined solely as a freshman player in the big leagues—on the basis of his hitting, his running, his defensive play, his team value."

"We Were the Pioneers"

Few players from the Negro leagues are alive today. The major stars, including Paige, Gibson, Cool Papa Bell, and Jackie Robinson, had died by the end of the century. Sadly, while a handful of major black stars has been inducted into the Hall of Fame, thousands of other players, and along with them, the story of black baseball, have been shoved to the back pages of history. Few people know of their stories and deeds. Jackie Robinson came along, smashed the color barrier, and in the process so thoroughly nudged black baseball aside that many people think black

"Cool Papa" Bell is inducted into the Major League Baseball Hall of Fame in Cooperstown, New York, in 1974.

baseball started with Robinson. "I'd go out on the street and the kids didn't know a thing about our Negro baseball," [105] lamented Ray Dandridge, who played in the 1930s and 1940s. He and others found that their neighbors knew about Jackie Robinson and a small collection of other players, but little beyond that.

These men deserve to be remembered for more than just their athletic prowess. They laid the foundation upon which every future black baseball player built his career. They took a segregated society's abuse, they endured the mind-numbing hours on dilapidated buses and ate in run-down diners, they slept in tents or cars or fourth-rate hotels. Despite these obstacles, they succeeded, and by so doing sent the message to black youths that, if they possessed the same fiery spirit, they could succeed in their fields of endeavor.

"We never thought about the major leagues," said Gene Benson. "We never thought it would happen. We never dreamed that it would come true. But I know we were the pioneers. Without our league, where would Robinson have been drafted from? If we weren't out there suffering and struggling, they wouldn't have any blacks in there now." [106]

Without men like John Henry Lloyd and Buck O'Neil, Ray Dandridge and Chet Brewer, the path into the majors for Jackie Robinson and the men who followed him would have been more difficult.

By competing on an equal basis with white players on the occasions handed them through all-star games, the men of black baseball made it tougher for prejudiced minds to think the black man was inferior, and if that was true for baseball, it was true for any other endeavor in which black men and women hoped to excel. Black baseball helped the United States to become more fully integrated.

"The Jackies and the Ernies [Banks] changed things around; they changed the pattern for the black man," asserted Buck O'Neil. "I think sports, and baseball, did more for integration than anything did." [107]

"I Contributed Something"

Despite lingering tales that black athletes from the Negro leagues were bitter about not having the chance to play in the majors, very few harbored animosity over the situation. Most focus on the positive rather than dwell on the negatives. Judy Johnson, the great third baseman for Hilldale and the Pittsburgh Crawfords from 1921 to 1938, called his career "my happy days. I enjoyed every minute of it. If I had to live it over again, I would go over it again. I think it was worth living. It taught you to be a man and a gentleman in every respect. It taught you how to treat your fellow man." [108]

Whenever someone mentioned to shortstop John Henry Lloyd that he was born too soon, he had a ready retort: "I don't consider I was born at the wrong time. I feel it was the right time. I had a chance to prove the ability of our race in this sport, and because many of us did our best for the game, we've given the Negro a greater opportunity now to be accepted into the major leagues with other Americans." [109]

Buck O'Neil trumpeted the benefits he reaped from playing in the Negro leagues, even if it did mean the majors stood beyond his reach during his career:

> Born too soon? Forget it. You forget that. Waste no tears for me. I had a beautiful life. I played with the greatest ball players in the world, and I played against the best ball players in the world. I saw this country and a lot of other countries, and I met some wonderful people. They say, "Buck, you were born at the wrong time." I say, "No, I was born *right* on time."

Ex-Negro leagues player Ernie Banks accepts his second consecutive Most Valuable Player (MVP) award in 1959.

That's what surprises people about me. I'm not bitter. No. I don't have the bitter story. If I was going to be bitter about anything, it wouldn't be about baseball but about education. I have no idea what I could have been. Suppose I could have gone to Sarasota High School, the University of Florida. All these things I'll never know, about what kind of man I could have been.[110]

Finally, the men of black baseball know that even though they never stepped onto a major league field, they contributed to the betterment of the game and of society. For that, as well as for their athletic skills, they hope to be remembered.

"I have no ill feeling about never having had the opportunity to play in the big leagues," explained Jimmie Crutchfield:

There have been times—you know, they used to call me the Black Lloyd Waner. I used to think about that a lot. He was on the other side of town in Pittsburgh making $12,000 a year and I didn't have enough money to go home on. I had to borrow bus fare to come home.

It seemed like there was something wrong there. But that was yesterday. There's no use in me having bitterness in my heart this late in life about what's gone by. That's just the way I feel about it. Once in a while I get a kick out of thinking that my name was mentioned as one of the stars of the East-West game and little things like that. I don't know whether I'd feel better if I had a million dollars.

I can say I contributed something. [111]

Notes

Introduction: Two Realms

1. Quoted in Mark Ribowsky, *A Complete History of the Negro Leagues.* New York: Citadel Press, 2002, p. 22.
2. Quoted in Robert Peterson, *Only the Ball Was White.* Englewood Cliffs, NJ: Prentice-Hall, 1970, p. 39.
3. Quoted in Sol White, *Sol White's History of Colored Base Ball, with other Documents on the Early Black Game, 1886–1936.* Lincoln: University of Nebraska Press, 1995, p. 137.
4. Quoted in Ribowsky, *A Complete History of the Negro Leagues,* pp. 27–28.

Chapter 1: "I Learned Baseball the Hard Way"

5. Quoted in John B. Holway, *Black Diamonds: Life in the Negro Leagues from the Men Who Lived It.* Westport, CT: Meckler, 1989, p. 93.
6. Quoted in Peterson, *Only the Ball Was White,* p. 126.
7. Quoted in Peterson, *Only the Ball Was White,* p. 127.
8. Quoted in Donn Rogosin, *Invisible Men: Life in Baseball's Negro Leagues.* New York: Atheneum, 1983, p. 22.
9. Quoted in Holway, *Black Diamonds,* p. 72.
10. Quoted in Peterson, *Only the Ball Was White,* p. 81.
11. Quoted in Rogosin, *Invisible Men,* p. 73.
12. Quoted in Rogosin, *Invisible Men,* p. 76.
13. Quoted in Rogosin, *Invisible Men,* p. 76.
14. Quoted in Holway, *Black Diamonds,* p. 59.
15. Quoted in Rogosin, *Invisible Men,* p. 84.
16. Quoted in John B. Holway, *Voices from the Great Black Baseball Leagues.* New York: Dodd, Mead, 1975, p. 123.
17. Quoted in John B. Holway, *Blackball Stars: Negro League Pioneers.* Westport, CT: Meckler, 1988, p. 341.
18. Quoted in White, *History of Colored Base Ball,* p. 67.
19. Quoted in Peterson, *Only the Ball Was White,* p. 99.

Chapter 2: The Great Barnstorming Tours

20. Quoted in Ribowsky, *A Complete History of the Negro Leagues,* pp. 77–78.
21. Quoted in Holway, *Black Diamonds,* p. 24.
22. Frazier "Slow" Robinson, with Paul Bauer, *Catching Dreams: My Life in the Negro Baseball Leagues.* Syracuse, NY: Syracuse University Press, 1999, p. 18.
23. Quoted in Holway, *Blackball Stars,* p. 318.
24. Quoted in Holway, *Black Diamonds,* p. 80.
25. Quoted in Rogosin, *Invisible Men,* p. 143.
26. Quoted in Holway, *Black Diamonds,* p. 94.
27. Quoted in Ribowsky, *A Complete History of the Negro Leagues,* p. 89.
28. Quoted in William Brashler, *The Story of Negro League Baseball.* New York: Ticknor & Fields, 1994, pp. 66–67.
29. Quoted in Holway, *Black Diamonds,* p. 79.
30. Quoted in Ribowsky, *A Complete History of the Negro Leagues,* p. 84.
31. Quoted in Holway, *Blackball Stars,* p. 320.
32. Quoted in Holway, *Black Diamonds,* p. 25.
33. Quoted in Peterson, *Only the Ball Was White,* p. 155.
34. Quoted in Peterson, *Only the Ball Was White,* pp. 3–4.
35. Quoted in Holway, *Voices from the Great Black Baseball Leagues,* p. 131.
36. Quoted in Holway, *Black Diamonds,* p. 171.

37. Quoted in Holway, *Blackball Stars*, pp. 319–20.
38. Quoted in Ribowsky, *A Complete History of the Negro Leagues*, p. xix.
39. Quoted in Rogosin, *Invisible Men*, p. 79.

Chapter 3: "I Am a Man"

40. Quoted in Rogosin, *Invisible Men*, p. 27.
41. Quoted in Bruce Chadwick, *When the Game Was Black and White: The Illustrated History of the Negro Leagues*. New York: Abbeville Press, 1992, p. 132.
42. Quoted in Chadwick, *When the Game Was Black and White*, p. 153.
43. Quoted in Chadwick, *When the Game Was Black and White*, p. 135.
44. Quoted in Brashler, *The Story of Negro League Baseball*, p. 69.
45. Quoted in Rogosin, *Invisible Men*, p. 163.
46. Quoted in Rogosin, *Invisible Men*, p. 31.
47. Quoted in Chadwick, *When the Game Was Black and White*, pp. 147–49.
48. Quoted in Holway, *Black Diamonds*, p. 32.
49. Quoted in Holway, *Voices from the Great Black Baseball Leagues*, pp. 125–26.
50. Quoted in Rogosin, *Invisible Men*, p. 168.
51. Quoted in Ribowsky, *A Complete History of the Negro Leagues*, p. 219.
52. Robinson, *Catching Dreams*, p. 167.
53. Robinson, *Catching Dreams*, p. 184.
54. Quoted in Chadwick, *When the Game Was Black and White*, p. 153.

Chapter 4: "Black in a White World"

55. Quoted in Peterson, *Only the Ball Was White*, p. 23.
56. Quoted in Ribowsky, *A Complete History of the Negro Leagues*, pp. 28–29.
57. Quoted in Robinson, *Catching Dreams*, p. 17.
58. Quoted in Holway, *Black Diamonds*, p. 20.
59. Quoted in Peterson, *Only the Ball Was White*, p. 41.
60. Quoted in Peterson, *Only the Ball Was White*, p. 41.
61. Robinson, *Catching Dreams*, p. 61.
62. Quoted in Holway, *Black Diamonds*, p. 60.
63. Quoted in Holway, *Black Diamonds*, p. 59.
64. Quoted in Holway, *Black Diamonds*, pp. 59–60.
65. Quoted in Ribowsky, *A Complete History of the Negro Leagues*, p. 97.
66. Robinson, *Catching Dreams*, p. 61.
67. Quoted in Ribowsky, *A Complete History of the Negro Leagues*, p. xviii.
68. Quoted in Ribowsky, *A Complete History of the Negro Leagues*, p. 23.
69. Quoted in Ribowsky, *A Complete History of the Negro Leagues*, p. 85.
70. Quoted in Peterson, *Only the Ball Was White*, pp. 31–32.

Chapter 5: "They Knew There'd Be a Good Show"

71. Quoted in Ribowsky, *A Complete History of the Negro Leagues*, p. 243.
72. Leroy (Satchel) Paige, *Maybe I'll Pitch Forever: A Great Baseball Player Tells the Hilarious Story Behind the Legend*. Lincoln: University of Nebraska Press, 1993, p. 159.
73. Quoted in Ribowsky, *A Complete History of the Negro Leagues*, p. 184.
74. Quoted in Ribowsky, *A Complete History of the Negro Leagues*, p. 248.
75. Quoted in Holway, *Black Diamonds*, p. 153.
76. Quoted in Brashler, *The Story of Negro League Baseball*, p. 138.
77. Quoted in Holway, *Black Diamonds*, p. 71.
78. Quoted in Art Rust Jr., *"Get That Nigger off the Field!" A Sparkling, Informal History of the Black Man in Baseball*. New York: Delacorte Press, 1976, pp. 16–17.
79. Quoted in Ribowsky, *A Complete History of the Negro Leagues*, p. 236.

80. Quoted in Ribowsky, *A Complete History of the Negro Leagues*, p. 224.
81. Quoted in Brashler, *The Story of Negro League Baseball*, p. 101.
82. Quoted in Peterson, *Only the Ball Was White*, p. 158.
83. Quoted in Peterson, *Only the Ball Was White*, p. 160.
84. Buck O'Neil, with Steve Wulf and David Conrads, *I Was Right On Time.* New York: Simon & Schuster, 1996, p. 50.
85. Quoted in Rogosin, *Invisible Men*, p. 81.
86. Quoted in Brent P. Kelley, *Voices from the Negro Leagues: Conversations with 52 Baseball Standouts of the Period 1924–1960.* Jefferson, NC: McFarland, 1998, p. 223.

Chapter 6: "Somebody Has to Make the First Move"

87. Quoted in Brashler, *The Story of Negro League Baseball*, p. 116.
88. Quoted in Rogosin, *Invisible Men*, p. 198.
89. Quoted in Rogosin, *Invisible Men*, p. 181.
90. Quoted in Ribowsky, *A Complete History of the Negro Leagues*, p. 252.
91. Quoted in Brashler, *The Story of Negro League Baseball*, pp. 118–19.
92. Quoted in Peterson, *Only the Ball Was White*, p. 178.
93. Quoted in Ribowsky, *A Complete History of the Negro Leagues*, pp. 252–253.
94. Quoted in Rogosin, *Invisible Men*, p. 19.
95. Quoted in Rogosin, *Invisible Men*, p. 197.
96. Quoted in Peterson, *Only the Ball Was White*, p. 176.
97. Quoted in Peterson, *Only the Ball Was White*, p. 183.
98. Quoted in Ribowsky, *A Complete History of the Negro Leagues*, p. 280.
99. Robinson, *Catching Dreams*, pp. 104, 123.
100. Quoted in Ribowsky, *A Complete History of the Negro Leagues*, p. xvii.
101. Quoted in Holway, *Black Diamonds*, p. 142.
102. Robinson, *Catching Dreams*, p. 184.
103. Quoted in Brashler, *The Story of Negro League Baseball*, p. 146.
104. Quoted in Holway, *Black Diamonds*, p. xi.
105. Quoted in Rogosin, *Invisible Men*, p. 219.
106. Quoted in Holway, *Black Diamonds*, p. 85.
107. Quoted in Holway, *Black Diamonds*, p. 103.
108. Quoted in Brashler, *The Story of Negro League Baseball*, p. 153.
109. Quoted in Holway, *Blackball Stars*, pp. 319–47.
110. Quoted in Holway, *Black Diamonds*, p. 104.
111. Quoted in Peterson, *Only the Ball Was White*, pp. 204–205.

For Further Reading

Books

Janet Bruce, *The Kansas City Monarchs: Champions of Black Baseball.* Lawrence: University Press of Kansas, 1985. The story of the Kansas City Monarchs, one of black baseball's top franchises, is thoroughly told in this book.

Wilmer Fields, *My Life in the Negro Leagues: An Autobiography.* Westport, CT: Meckler, 1992. A player in the 1940s, Fields describes his days with the Homestead Grays and other teams.

Brent P. Kelley, *"I Will Never Forget": Interviews with 39 Former Negro League Players.* Jefferson, NC: McFarland, 2003. Kelley has devoted his career to capturing the stories of Negro league players. This book contains thirty-nine interviews, mostly dealing with the era following Jackie Robinson.

Michael E. Lomax, *Black Baseball Entrepreneurs, 1860–1901.* Syracuse, NY: Syracuse University Press, 2003. Lomax traces the origins of black baseball and describes how it evolved into a full-fledged business.

Patricia C. McKissack and Frederick McKissack Jr., *Black Diamond: The Story of the Negro Baseball Leagues.* New York: Scholastic, 1994. A fine summary of the black baseball leagues. The chapters on the origins of black baseball and on playing in Latin America are particularly good.

Walter Dean Myers, *The Journal of Biddy Owens, the Negro Leagues.* New York: Scholastic, 2001. A fictionalized diary of an African-American playing in Negro baseball of the 1940s. The book illustrates life on the road for the players.

James Overmyer, *Effa Manley and the Newark Eagles.* Metuchen, NJ: Scarecrow Press, 1993. Effa Manley's role in the Negro leagues is examined in this book by Overmyer. The wife of the Eagles' owner, Effa Manley took an active part in running the team.

James A. Riley, *The Negro Leagues.* New York: Chelsea House, 1997. Junior high school students will enjoy Riley's survey of the Negro leagues. The author explains black baseball from its origins to 1960.

Web Sites

Blackbaseball.com (www.blackbaseball.com). This site has facts, books, and merchandise related to the Negro leagues.

National Baseball Hall of Fame (www.baseballhalloffame.org). The official Web site of the baseball Hall of Fame in Cooperstown, New York. Some of the Negro leagues best players, such as Satchel Paige, Josh Gibson, and Cool Papa Bell, are profiled here.

Negro League Baseball Players Association (www.nlbpa.com). This Web site features player profiles, team logos, news updates on former players and more.

Negro League Baseball: Out of the Shadows (www.outoftheshadows.net). This site contains a history of the Negro leagues, as well as player biographies.

The Negro Leagues Museum (www.nlbm .com). The museum, located in Kansas City, Missouri, is run by former Negro leagues great Buck O'Neill. The Web site contains pictures, a history of the Negro leagues, and player profiles.

Works Consulted

Books

William Brashler, *The Story of Negro League Baseball*. New York: Ticknor & Fields, 1994. This book provides a helpful examination of the origins and contributions of black baseball and the men who played it. Numerous photographs complement a fine text.

———, *Josh Gibson: A Life in the Negro Leagues*. New York: Harper & Row, 1978. Brashler delivers the only decent biography of Josh Gibson. He helps the reader understand this talented, yet ultimately troubled man.

Bruce Chadwick, *When the Game Was Black and White: The Illustrated History of the Negro Leagues*. New York: Abbeville Press, 1992. Any reader will delight in Chadwick's survey of Negro baseball. He intersperses numerous photographs among the nuggets of information that dominate his chapters.

John B. Holway, *Blackball Stars: Negro League Pioneers*. Westport, CT: Meckler, 1988. Holway has compiled a superb collection of brief biographies of Negro leagues players, including Oscar Charleston and John Henry Lloyd.

———, *Black Diamonds: Life in the Negro Leagues from the Men Who Lived It*. Westport, CT: Meckler, 1989. This fascinating book contains the reminiscences of eleven black stars, giving insight into the life and talents of these under-appreciated men.

———, *Voices from the Great Black Baseball Leagues*. New York: Dodd, Mead, 1975. Holway's initial contribution to Negro baseball remains as valuable today as it was thirty years ago. In the book, he interviews eighteen major stars from those long-ago days.

Brent P. Kelley, *Voices from the Negro Leagues: Conversations with 52 Baseball Standouts of the Period 1924–1960*. Jefferson, NC: McFarland, 1998. Kelley interviewed fifty-two players from the Negro leagues to compile this useful volume of oral history.

Buck Leonard, with James A. Riley, *Buck Leonard: The Black Lou Gehrig: The Hall of Famer's Story in His Own Words*. New York: Carroll & Graf, 1995. Leonard, a member of baseball's Hall of Fame, traces his career from his childhood until his induction at Cooperstown.

Buck O'Neil, with Steve Wulf and David Conrads, *I Was Right On Time*. New York: Simon & Schuster, 1996. A great player in his own right, Buck O'Neil offers insights and commentary on black baseball and on the talented stars who performed in the days of separate leagues.

Leroy (Satchel) Paige, *Maybe I'll Pitch Forever: A Great Baseball Player Tells the Hilarious Story Behind the Legend*. Lincoln: University of Nebraska Press, 1993. Paige's colorful account of his life almost matches the colorfulness of his career. This autobiography is indispensable for gaining an understanding of Paige and of black baseball.

Robert Peterson, *Only the Ball Was White*. Englewood Cliffs, NJ: Prentice-Hall, 1970. Peterson broke new ground with his heralded history of the Negro leagues. His book, the first of its type, explored the origins and impact of black baseball. He also includes a large section containing brief biographies of some of the most prominent black players.

Mark Ribowsky, *A Complete History of the Negro Leagues*. New York: Citadel Press, 2002. Ribowsky has written a very thorough history of black baseball in the United States. The narrative slows when he focuses on the business and political moves by team owners, but he compensates by including many fascinating anecdotes.

Frazier "Slow" Robinson, with Paul Bauer, *Catching Dreams: My Life in the Negro Baseball Leagues*. Syracuse, NY: Syracuse University Press, 1999. Robinson's memoir of his baseball days contains a few good glimpses of life in black baseball, but relies too much on his recollections of different players.

Donn Rogosin, *Invisible Men: Life in Baseball's Negro Leagues*. New York: Atheneum, 1983. This is one of the finest histories of life in black baseball. Rogosin's chapters of life on the road, playing baseball in Latin America, and the march toward integration proved particularly helpful.

Art Rust Jr., *"Get That Nigger off the Field!" A Sparkling, Informal History of the Black Man in Baseball*. New York: Delacorte Press, 1976. Rust's examination of black baseball yields numerous fascinating stories and revealing quotes. The author's background as a sports announcer helped prepare him for the task.

Jules Tygiel, *Past Time: Baseball as History*. New York: Oxford University Press, 2000. Tygiel's nine chapters on baseball history include an excellent one dealing with baseball during the segregation years.

Sol White, *Sol White's History of Colored Base Ball, with Other Documents on the Early Black Game, 1886–1936*. Lincoln: University of Nebraska Press, 1995. First published in 1907, White's groundbreaking book provides a powerful, and often moving, examination into the origins of black baseball. A fan of any age will love reading this volume.

Videos

"Only the Ball Was White." Chicago: WTTW-TV, 1992. Includes interviews of greats, such as Satchel Paige, Buck Leonard, and David Malarcher.

"There Was Always Sun Shining Someplace," produced and directed by Craig Davidson. Westport, CT: Refocus Films, 1984. Interviews with Cool Papa Bell, Judy Johnson, and Monte Irvin make this documentary valuable.

Index

Picture Credits

Cover: © Bettmann/CORBIS

© Bettmann/CORBIS, 26, 33, 37, 38, 41, 42, 45, 51, 55, 60, 62, 70, 72, 75, 77, 84, 88, 89, 94

© CORBIS, 11

MLB Photos via Getty Images, 29, 69

© Museum of the City of New York/CORBIS, 58

National Baseball Hall of Fame Library, Cooperstown, N.Y., 12, 13, 14, 15, 18, 20, 22, 23, 24, 32, 35, 46, 48, 50, 53, 59, 64, 79, 80, 83, 86, 92

Time-Life Pictures/Getty Images, 28

© Underwood & Underwood/CORBIS, 65

About the Author

John F. Wukovits is a junior high school teacher and writer from Trenton, Michigan, who specializes in history and biography. Besides biographies of Anne Frank, Jim Carrey, Michael J. Fox, Stephen King, and Martin Luther King Jr. for Lucent, he has written biographies of the World War II commander Adm. Clifton Sprague, Barry Sanders, Tim Allen, Jack Nicklaus, Vince Lombardi, and Wyatt Earp. He is also the author of many books about World War II, including *Pacific Alamo: The Battle for Wake Island.* A graduate of the University of Notre Dame, Wukovits is the father of three daughters—Amy, Julie, and Karen.